DECLINING UNITED STATES
THE RISING
REPUBLIC OF CHINA

James A. Hudson

ISBN 978-1-953223-03-6 (paperback)

Copyright © 2020 by James A. Hudson

All rights reserved. No part of this publication may be reproduced, distributed, or transmitted in any form or by any means, including photocopying, recording, or other electronic or mechanical methods without the prior written permission of the publisher. For permission requests, solicit the publisher via the address below.

Rushmore Press LLC
1 800 460 9188
www.rushmorepress.com

Printed in the United States of America

DEDICATION

To my beautiful caring wife, Donna, you been very supportive in going the extra mile to see that my requirements are met. I thank you for your loyalty, support, and tender loving care (TLC) over the years we have been together. I couldn't have done many of the things that I did without your help and assistance.

And so, I take pleasure in dedicating this book to you, our children, and the Hudson family.

I wish all of you good health, good luck, good success, and prosperity. I want you to know that I love and admire all of you. Please do good work/continue to do good work, and stay out of trouble, and away from conflict.

Remember, where there is no vision (foresight), the people shall be sure to perish. As such, you should have a clear vision as to where you want to go, what you want to do, and work at it. Always be on the right side, think before you act, and stay focus on whatever you are doing.

Indeed, the winding roads of this life has many twists and turns. It has led us to where we are at this point in time. We won some, and we lost some. However, we are still here—we are alive and well /not so well? In any event, we are victors rather than victims! You should be aware of the fact that in this life we may encounter trials, troubles, and tribulations. God forbid, if and when you should be inflicted with any of these scourge, you should remember to bear up nobly under any and all adversities.

Therefore, let's give thanks, let's rejoice, let's lift up our voice and sing.

May you be blessed.

CONTENTS

Acknowledgment 7
Introduction..9
Chapter 1:   The All-Seeing Eyes of the Providence......................19
Chapter 2:   Messages from Divine Providence............................36
Chapter 3:   Declining United States, the Rising China. 55
Chapter 4:   Rise and Fall of Empires..76
Chapter 5:   No Profit, No Gain: Exploring Distant Planets 93
Chapter 6:   Early American History..104
Chapter 7:   Black Americans' Contribution To History.............119
Chapter 8:   Motivational Assistance to the Left Behind.............134
Chapter 9:   Providential Command to the Human Race...........160
Chapter 10: The Rising Republic of China 171
Words of Wisdom and Inspiration 181
Conclusion..189

ACKNOWLEDGMENT

To the families, friends, and loved ones of those who perished in the destruction of the World Trade Centers in New York City on September11, 2001, I am sorry for your loss. This book is for you. To the first responders - fire fighters, police officers, medical personnel - I offer my deepest sympathies. Many of these brave men and women did their jobs that day and are still with us. Many are inflicted with chronic diseases and respiratory ailments as a result of exposure to toxic chemicals and polluted air. This book is an expression of gratitude, compassion, and love.

These calamities by Islamic terrorists on the United Stated could have been avoided. Nevertheless, we learned valuable lessons from the attack. The truth is, similar attacks in this country have been avoided in this country since then. May similar things never ever happen again.It's true, there is no safe place on this earth. No man knows what will befall him, in terms of adversities, calamities, and troubles. Many leave their houses and return impaired, while many others never return home again. It is a fact, the future is not ours to see, our destiny is hidden in the memory of the universe, and with father time.And so, a word of advice to the wise. I encourage my readers, and others, to be prudent in all their undertakings. Remember, tomorrow is promised to no man. We can be here today, and gone tomorrow. As such, keep the insurance policies for yourself and your loved ones up to date. In any event, before you leave the house please say a little prayer for your family, your friends, and for yourself.God bless you, and God bless America.

INTRODUCTION

The declining of the United States and the rising of the Republic of Red China is discussed in this book. Each chapter will be supportive of the case I have presented. Each chapter will place emphases on different element that is contributing to the declining process. I make the case and presented the evidence, you will be the Judge.

Communist Russia has lost its title as the 'second superpower' behind the United States. On the other hand, all indication indicates that our superpower status is coming into question. As the U.S superpower status comes into question, it's important to take not of the malfeasance in this country and of the similarity between its part and those of former world superpowers: Egypt, Greece, Rome, and England. And so I reached a brief and fundamental histories of these countries mentioned above.

The United States seems to have reached the pinnacle in terms of wealth, power, and prestige, and failed to remain at that peak. It failed to remain on the summit, and it's descending at a rate that's questionable. Rapidly, or gradually, that's the question. The answer to the question depends on what side of the 'spectrum' you are. Certainly, the current trend across the nation seems to suggest that the prognoses are authentic. There are political retribution and strife, voice, hatred, among others things that are contributing to eroding America's superpower status. People in other parts of the world are in disbelief in connection with the things that are taking place in this country. These things are discussed in this book.

As a gifted visionary it's my duty to reveal things that many aren't aware of and are hidden below the surface. I will not be held accountable by God, and nature's gods for concealing the truth. I leave accountability to those in the news media. Many Journalists and others in the news reporting sectors will not bring good news. For the most part, many are bearers of bad news, distortion, and propaganda. In many cases they are supporters of political parties of their choice and they support the 'narrative'.

America and the American people face many perils and troubles. The question is, are we on a path to self-destruction and cultural decline? Many believed that to be the case.

From a political standpoint the nation is deeply divided. One side proclaimed that they are right and the other is wrong, the other side disagreed, "no we are right and your side is wrong". Well, there are two sides to things but the truth is somewhere in the center. In the meantime, animosity, retribution, and discord continue.

With all this mess taking place across the country Red China will be at par with the United States before long. Then at some point in the not too distant future China will overtake the United States and will become the next superpower.

Red China isn't experiencing many of the ills that are facing American society. Their people seem to be disciplined, productive, and sober. Besides, their government is lifting those at the lower end of the economic level out of poverty and ignorance. They are educating their people. Currently, there are more middle class Chinese than middle-class Americans. I will present the facts as they relate to the disappearing middle class Americans. In fact, the masses have been kept in ignorance and darkness. This mode is advantageous to the elite, the ruling class, and the wealthy.

Political unrest, crime, the use of mind-altering substance abuse, among other things of this nature, are unheard of in Communist China. I will look into the Chinese society to find what they are doing right. They must have been doing things right to be challenging the United States. We must find the answer to the question and make the necessary correction.

Many around the globe and in this country believe that the American society and culture are waning. That seems to be the case. Politics is a major factor in terms of division and unrest. However, there are far more serious issues across the country that's contributing to the destablilization than politics. I will address them in the book.

From a cultural standpoint, how long can American culture remain intact? There are no English speaking people migrating from other nations who are not assimilating in American culture. I am not disparaging others from countries that don't speak English as their language. The question is, how are they going to function effectively in an English speaking America, at least for the immediate future? In the immediate future, since the English language will eventually become the second, or even third language if the current trend continues. Indeed, America is moving in a direction that's questionable.

With the declining birthrate of European Americans, and the rising of non-English speaking ethnic groups/races, it will be a matter of time before the language of the foreigners become the dominant ones. These, among other things, will be the beginning of the end of European civilization in America. In fact, the process is already in motion. I will take up this matter later.

Indeed, the cultural problems facing the nation and its people are many and varied. And so the collapse of the civilization is imminent. In this book I will bring to your attention to many issues that are contributing to these problems, and offer appropriate solutions. Many Americans are gripped with fear and uncertainty, in terms of the future, and rightfully so. As such, the hearts of the American ruling class, elite, and others, are troubled.

In connection with global warming issues, how long will the earth endure if these things continue? The earth is taking a pounding and this should be of concern to all. In terms of this pounding, there are all sorts of controversy in connection with the global warming phenomenon. I will present Divine revelation in connection with global warming issues in the appropriate chapter. Providence made startling revelations in connection with the troubles facing this planet and its inhabitants. You will read these revelations for yourself in this book! In fact, the powers governing the earth aren't pleased with the people on this planet. You will read their comments in the chapter. One thing is clear-- the powers governing the universe are watching.

In connection with the celestial spheres, there are numerous planets, stars, and moons in the solar system. They are constantly radiating invisible waves to the earth. It should be noted that humans have constantly been exposed to radiations from the above-mentioned. In fact, we are being influenced by these celestial waves and many people aren't aware of them. Everyone should understand the dynamics behind the planets in the heavens.

The question is, are these waves from distant planets, stars, and moons detrimental to humans and animals? These may have been some of the contributing factors in terms of the behavior of humans and animals in this country and across the globe. Understanding these phenomena are important. Educational enlightenment in these matters are the key for preventing one from going off the rails as they say. We must understand the effects of these planets on the minds of people. We will look into these matters as well.

People must pay close attention to the influence external sources are having on our minds since we are in tune with good and evil sources. Think of all the radiation we are being expose to constantly. It's no wonder many go crazy and bring vengeance on others.

On the other hand, America (United States) was founded and built on Julio-Christian principles. Why is there so much upheaval within our society and with our people? Many are at their wit's end, explaining the reasons behind these dynamics that are taking place across the nation and around the globe.

I am here to set the record straight and bring to the forefront the causes and effects behind the problems faced by this nation and its people, and also by people in other nations around the world. I will bring them to your attention in the chapters of the book.

In terms of US decline, are there solutions to reverse the many ills facing the nation and its people? Yes, there are. Every problem has a solution. Nevertheless, there are problems that people will not be able to solve themselves. People will not be able to resolve issues brought about by providential decree. In this case, people should summon the help of an offended God to intervene and bring about resolutions to many of the problems facing America and its people.

Now, whether the American people are willing and ready to apply these solutions for the resolution of the nation's troubles is another matter. But it should be clear that people will not be able to remove misfortune brought about by Divine Providence. These solutions lie in petitioning the realms of Divine Providence for the cure. Please see below quotations from the Holy book.

"If my people, which are called by my name, shall humble themselves, and pray, and seek my face, and turn from their wicked ways, then will I hear from heaven, and will forgive their sins, and will heal their land." (2 Chronicles 7:1400)

Are we willing to do these things in bringing healing to this nation?

Cain and Abel

For those who aren't grounded in scriptures, I will bring the story of Cain and Abel to your attention. Cain slaughtered his brother Abel out of jealousy and envy. Cain was cursed by the Divine for the evil he had done. This curse is still in effect. This curse has affected / is affecting the descendants of Cain throughout the ages to this day. These are some of the dynamics playing out across this nation today. In fact, these things will continue until the curse of Cain is broken.

And so, I am calling on people of all regions and faiths to petition the higher powers governing the universe to mercifully nullify the curse on the descendants of Cain. Until this is reversed, destruction will not cease.

We will look at other factors relative to the misfortune brought about by disobeying the laws of the universe. It should be noted that stealing, killing, adultery, and other misdeeds don't go unnoticed by the higher powers. You cannot see them, you cannot hear them, but they are there!

JAMES A. HUDSON

The Jewish People and Christianity

Contrary to popular opinion, it wasn't the Jews that crucified Christ as many would have you believe. The prosecution of the Jewish people goes back to ancient Egypt. In addition, their ancestors placed bad blessings on them during the crucifixion of Jesus. We will study their history to determine the cause and effect behind their constant prosecution. The Jews around the globe are experiencing a common enemy; 'blood curse'!

In terms of atrocities brought about by people, there is no end in sight. The question of where and to whom Mr. Bad will bring his vengeance in the near future is uppermost in the hearts and minds of many Americans and others. Even children at the school age level are bringing vengeance on others. Remember, people are constantly being indluenced by external sources of which they are not aware, and have little control over. These are some of the dynamics at work all over the globe! Reading this book will bring awareness, in terms of understanding the nature of external sources and influences on the mind.

Benevolent source doesn't inspire/influence people into violence or nefarious activities. In any event, the benevolent source is the source that people should cherish and seek to align themselves with. I repeat, as a Christian nation, we should accept all things originating from the source of all good and reject all things that fall into the realm of the malevolent sphere.

It's true, evil dynamics are undermining our success and ability to unite as Americans. These things will affect America's abilities to produce and lead as a world superpower. If we are united, we will stand. If we are divided as a nation and as a people, we will fall. It appears as though the latter is taking a toll. If we fall as a nation, it will be from within. We the people will not be guiltless; we will have to take the blame. In terms of unity, we must set aside our differences and unite. Unity is strength, and division is a sign of weakness. The world is watching us to see where we are going next as a nation. In the meantime, developing nations are waiting to dethrone America as the next superpower.

Please note that malevolent forces that originated in the dark domain are getting the better of this nation and its people. Evil things that took place many decades ago are suddenly resurfacing, appearing out of the blue, and bringing down mighty and powerful men. Mighty men are being brought down by those who were once thought to be insignificant and less important in society.

We must wake up and exorcise the demons that originated in the realm of darkness. Let's drive nefarious forces from among us so that peace, happiness, prosperity, and good health may dwell in our homes and follow us and our children/grandchildren throughout our lives, and their lives. Again, this nation is under attack from diverse sources. Sitting and doing nothing is the wrong approach. The poem below will help you understand those nefarious forces that our nation and its people are up against, and the solutions necessary:

I. *Cause and effect: see the mighty host advancing, Satan leading on mighty men around us are falling courage almost gone.*
II. *Solution: see the glorious banner waving hear the trumpet blow in our leader's name we'll triumphant over every foe. Farce and long the battle rages But our help is near Onward comes our great Commander, Cheer, my comrades cheer!*

Note: this is a poem from one of my collections in a 4.5x4,23 page novel that I brought with me from Jamaica. It is the best gift I ever received. It is decades old yet relevant today as never before. I will revisit this in another chapter.

The Best Gift

As mentioned, this book of poems is the best gift I ever received! The best gifts last a long time, bring real joy, can be freely shared with others, and make a difference in our lives. The best gifts are not trivial. They penetrate the surface, have deep meaning, and last long after we are gone. And so, these words of inspiration and wisdom that I will share with you will last a lifetime. They can be found in the chapter of the book.

Yes, we can triumph over the forces of darkness that are plaguing this nation and its people. This nation was founded on Christian principles, and we are supposed to be Christian—or are we? I leave you to be the judge in this matter.

Are the inhabitants of earth being affected by negative waves that originated in distant planets? This is entirely possible as mentioned. We will look into these things and let you be the judge.

In terms of poverty, the United States is supposed to be the wealthiest nation on earth. Yet, there is poverty everywhere. Those at the lower end of the economic spectrum should be lifted up out of poverty. The question is, how should this nation go about lifting people out of poverty, hopelessness, and despair? There are many ways to go about it. One of them is by educating the masses. We should teach people how to lift themselves out of poverty, hopelessness, and despair. We will address these issues in this book.

It should be noted that a wealthy New York businessman running for the 2020 presidential election spent over $357 million of his own money between January and February 16, 2020. According to a reliable source, the candidate has spent $260 million on broadcast TV, $24 million on cable, $9 million on radio and $64 million on digital, for a total of $357 million.

Now, think of the many poor kids that could have been helped with the money. They could have been helped by giving them the opportunities to go to schools and learn marketable skills. But no, politics is given preference over the less fortunate in this case. Heaven helps us all.

We will look at the decline of previous empires to determine the common thread that runs between them and the troubles facing this nation and its people. There are many parallels that can be drawn between the decline of the Roman Empire—and other empires— and the decline facing the United States. The Roman Empire lasted for around 1,500 years before it collapsed. How long will American civilization last?

Many people talk about greed and selfishness. In this country, there is no shortage of selfishness, greed, and arrogance. I was listening to a talk radio station recently, and I was pleasantly surprised at a comment made by a well-respected lawyer: "We lawyers run this country—we still do—and we make the laws so they are advantageous to us." We will get back to this statement later, but his comment speaks for itself.

The powers controlling the universe are not pleased with humanity. Providence is discussed with people, not just here in this country but across the globe. "Regarding the behavior of your fellowmen, a humbleness, a beauty needs to come in to replace the arrogance and greed, and it will be so." This Providential decree, among others, are presented in the book! I will present the revelation in the appropriate chapter. The secrets and mysteries will be revealed to you. However, you should understand that Mother Earth, Gaia, is in trouble. To combat the malfeasance facing the earth, Providence is working on things we humans cannot understand.

The poles are tilting. The North and South Poles are shifting. This results in colder weather coming to some areas, and other regions will experience warmer weather than usual. You will read about these startling Divine revelation in this book. In fact, the earth is in the process of a rebirth according to Providence. Please formalize yourself with the Providential instructions presented in this book.

People in the news media are duty bound to bring Providential message to the public. If they failed, they will be held accountable! (see chapter 2: pages 38 to 42)

Providential Revelation

The question of greed and arrogance by humans is well known. Providence is not pleased with these things. You will read more in this book in connection with Providential revelations. These things cannot be allowed to continue, change will be instituted by the elements, declared by divine providence! These revelations go on to reveal "overpopulation of the earth, plundering of the seas, pollution of the air," among other things were cited.

It's not clear as to what action will be taken to reduce the population of the earth. Could it be by way of plague, famine, incurable disease, or nuclear war propagated by the hands of people? Whichever way, the inhabitants of this planet should take note.

Frankly, people on this planet should be concerned. One thing is certain and it is that when Providence speaks people should take note!

Angels /Guardian Angels

How much do you know about angels/guardians angels? Guardian angels are celestial beings, and everyone were assigned a guardian angel at their birth. Yet, many go through life ignorant of this profound truth. If you aren't aware of your guardian angel, I will teach you about your guardian angels in this book. They are messengers between earth and Heaven. You have a duty, and responsibility to learn about your guardian angels. If you are interested, I can teach you about your protecting angel!

Without further ado, please allow me to bring this introduction to a close. This book will bring a wealth of information to you. And so, I am pleased to bring your attention to a book that brings the truth to light.

CHAPTER 1

The All-Seeing Eyes of the Providence

The universe is quite a mysterious place. For those who haven't fully grasped the concept when referencing the universe, we aren't referring to the earth alone. The earth is a tiny planet residing in what is known as the *terrestrial sphere*. We are also referring to the planets in outer regions of space, including Mars, Saturn, and Venus, etc. These planets reside in the *celestial sphere* or the *heavenly realms*. If we understood a fraction of the functioning of the universe, we would be wise and upright in all deportment. We would be cognizant of the higher power behind the smooth functioning and regulating of the universe.

Before we continue, you should understand a minor aspect of the universe as it relates to the troubles facing this nation. The universe is not a static place, thing, or entity. The universe is very dynamic. If we could see what is taking place in the ether, we would go crazy. There are many questions regarding the origin of the universe including the origin of the universe, why we are here, are there lives on other planets, etc. The answers to these and other secrets and mysteries are there. Whatever secrets and mysteries there are to be known will be revealed. Secrets and mysteries that are to be hidden will remain hidden.

In connection with the all-seeing eyes, we may refer to these eyes as *God, a universal power*, or the *Supreme Being*. The terminology used to describe these all-seeing eyes makes no difference. However, since we are supposed to be a Christian nation, in the United States, we refer to these eyes or this power as God, the Lord, or the Almighty. This is the deity that people should align themselves with if it is their desire to gain wisdom, knowledge, and understanding.

King Solomon of ancient Israel said, "The fear of the Lord is the beginning of wisdom." That is, wisdom in connection with spiritual and divine things.

The Powers Governing the Universe

The wise Creator created the universe and delegated its smooth functioning to the angelical beings. This is akin to a King delegating duty to his officials. These angelic beings are divided in hierarchy of angels as follows: the first hierarchy is made up of Seraphim, Cherubin, and Thrones; the second is made up of Domination, Quality, and Powers; the third is made up of Principalities, Archangels, angels and your own guardian angels. Your guardian angels are there to look over your destiny. You will find additional information in connection with guardian angels in chapter 2.

These angelic beings oversee the functioning of the universe as follows: that the planets remain in their orbits and not collide with others, that the earth's seasons are constant, and that seed-times and harvest doesn't cease, that the sea remains in its appointed boundary, etc. In effect, these beings regulate the smooth functioning of Mother mature. In effect, they are nature's gods.

There are millions of these angelic beings. You will not see them, you will not hear them, but they are there! If someone does something wrong, they will not be struck down on the spot, but they will be held accountable. On the other hand, if someone does good deeds, they will be rewarded. Please note that reward can present itself in different ways: good health, good relationships with others, success in life, financial blessing -- the possibilities are endless.

And so, now that I revealed these secrets and mystery, let's continue with the presentation. Someone who fears the Lord, is in good standing with other people, and is just and upright in all deportment, is probably on their way to true wisdom. Christians and others who are religiously inclined should possess some degree of wisdom. This is based on the fact that it's the Lord that is the source of true wisdom. In fact, those who fear the Lord, and give reverence to the Almighty Maker, should possess some degree of wisdom. But this is often not the case. In some cases, the opposite is the case.

What Percentage of Americans Believe in a God?

I am convinced that all wrongs and nefarious activities are due to lack of knowledge related to the functioning of the universe and a belief in the existence of a Supreme Being. I don't believe anyone would knowingly forfeit their right to a peaceful, happy, and prosperous existence by intentionally bringing harm to others and themselves. People often engage in evil activities simple because they aren't aware of the consequences that will follow. They aren't aware that there is no secret that can be hidden in the universe. Every act is seen and recorded. We will be rewarded for our good deeds and punished for our evil deeds. Christianity emphasizes these things, yet many ignorant people fail to do good instead of evil.

Before we continue, you should understand that the influence of distant planets in the far reaches of outer space is profound. They seem to have an effect on all living things on earth. There are people who believed that lunacy is pervasive at the time of the full moon. These things—and more—will be brought to your attention later in this book. In the meantime, let's contemplate the universe and the mind governing the universe.

The Universal Mind

The universe seems to have a mind of its own. The universe also seems to have eyes and ears; it sees and hears everything. Above all, this universe rewards and punishes us for the things we have done and for the things we have failed to do—with no exception. These things apply to mortals and to organizations, cities, towns, states, and nations. Nothing escapes the all-seeing eyes and ears of this universe.

The universe seems to have some sort of memory bank for storing and retrieving all kinds of information. Could this information be stored on distant planets in the celestial sphere of the heavenly bodies? Actions that have taken place since the beginning of time are recorded in universal memory. The universe works, and it delivers. This should be evident in terms of the situations taking place in this country.

Death will not extricate a soul from the good or evil that it committed during life. For the wrongs that one committed during life, one will pay even beyond the grave.

People are being rewarded or punished for their actions, words, and deeds on a daily basis. There is no escape from the eyes and ears of the universe. Sooner or later, people will reap their just rewards or negative karma. These are some of the secrets and mysteries of the universe that humans should be aware of. If this were the case, then the world would be more peaceful. There would be less crime, less violence, less evil, and fewer nefarious activities committed by the human race. We are hoping that once these secrets and mysteries are revealed, people will heed the warning and govern themselves accordingly.

The troubles facing this nation and its people are simply the universal laws at work. Many of you may fail to recognize this, but it's true. Things that happened decades ago that were stored in the memory of the universe have now been revealed or will be revealed. Hidden things are now coming to the light of day and will be coming to light in due time. This is the way of Providence.

Unfortunately, whenever the universe is dispensing retribution, there are those who bring harm to themselves. Nevertheless, the act of hurting oneself will not extricate the soul from its deeds.

It should be clear to everyone that there is such a thing as karma. This karma will fulfill its mission in this life or in the next. Ignorance of the workings of Providential law and the functioning of the universe is no excuse. Not knowing the danger associated with electricity will not prevent one from been killed if it is applied or used wrongly. And so, the consequences of disobeying providential laws are no different.

Based on all of the above, we encourage our fellow humans to be upright. Be upright and be just to your follow humans. Do good to all people for as long as you shall live. Remember the following:

> *For I, the Lord your God, am a jealous God, punishing the children for the fathers' sins, to the third and fourth generation of those who hate Me, but showing love to a thousand generations of those who love Me and keep my commandments. (Exodus 20:5)*

Benevolences are some of the attributes that promote inner peace, contentment, and harmony. You also shouldn't forget charity. Charity is an attribute of the Divine, and no good deeds will go unnoticed by the higher power. Above all, you should venerate the Almighty Maker. People who are born of a woman have but a short time on the planet, and it is full of misery. In time, everyone will return home to the place where souls originate to meet the Almighty Maker.

People should recognize the existence of God, the Supreme Being. These are some of the things that religions, including Christianity, have taught through the ages. However, many people have failed to recognize the concept. Many engage in destructive activities, believing that it's all over when they are dead. Nothing could be further from the truth. In time, this concept will become clear to nonbelievers.

I cannot overemphasize the concept of karma. It should never be forgotten that the law of karma is at work 24/7. Karmic law dictates that we will reap whatever we have sown—whether it's good or evil. How can one be aware of universal truth and still engage in all sorts of unsavory behavior, such as armed robbery, rape, or taking the life of another human? In my opinion, it's plain ignorance, among other things. Other things include insanity, influence by malevolent forces, and even influence from sources such as the moon. Let's continue by contemplating the planets in outer space—the celestial domain.

The Celestial Domain

There are many planets, stars, and moons in the solar system. Many have been discovered, and many are still to be discovered. I would like to touch briefly on the five major planets, one star, and one satellite that are of major importance to humans, animals, and other creatures on our planet. We should be mindful of the moon, Mars, Mercury, Jupiter, Venus, Saturn, and the sun. They are constantly beaming invisible rays to the surface of the earth. Could these planets be sending infrared rays that are affecting the human race? This could be the case. How else can we explain the irrationality of people's behavior in the United States and around the globe. Humans, animals, and plants are exposed to planetary radiation on a constant basis. Some of these rays are beneficial, but some are not. We will look into these things as we continue.

In terms of *universal memories*, you are aware that nothing that is hidden will remain hidden forever. There is evidence of this in recent sexual harassment cases and other things of these nature. Let's explore this matter as we continue.

Hidden Things Are Coming to Light

The United States is being rocked with scandals of unimaginable proportions. Many of these allegations and convictions for rape or unwanted sexual advances transpired many decades ago. It should be a reminder that whatever happened—good or evil—will eventually be brought to the light of day. The eyes of the universe and universal memories will bring hidden secrets to light and dispense rewards or punishments.

Time remembers all things that have transpired since the beginning of time. This is the reason why honesty, justice, and integrity are important. Allegations in connection with unwanted sexual behaviors by men are coming to the surface in no uncertain ways. Powerful men who were thought to be invincible are being brought down by women who were thought to be insignificant. As unfortunate as these things may seem, it's the universe at work. The universe is repaying karma to those who had taken advantage of those who were vulnerable and defenseless.

Every action has a reaction. Every unjust action has negative karmic consequences. People across the globe should be cognizant of the fact that what goes around comes around.

The hidden rape and sexual harassment suffered by women are only one aspect of the wrongs that are coming to light. There are other hidden dynamics that are coming to light for all to see. Please don't be alarmed in connection with things that will be revealed and brought to light in the near future in our beloved country.

In connection with sexual harassment, it should be noted that women are different from men. Men will never be able to understand the secret of women. Solomon, a wise person, confessed that he couldn't understand the secret of women. There is no point in men trying to understand women; they will not be able to. Just accept women for what they. There's no secret of women that will not revealed. Men, let caution be your guide in dealing with women. Ever since the beginning of time, women have been bringing men to their knees. Going back to biblical times, Samson and Delilah are a startling reminder of this dynamic.

My mother warned me many, many years ago that I should be careful with women since they are unreliable. She said, "Son, be careful in dealing with women. You should not reveal everything to them because when you fellas out with them, they will tell everything. They will reveal every one of your secrets."

The sexual harassment allegations reported by women against men are only creating animosity between the two genders on a corporate level. Tension is rising between the two groups in corporate America. The tension between the genders will play out in interesting ways. It is almost certain that sexual harassment allegations—true or false—will work to the disadvantage of women at all levels of society. This probably will result in excommunication of women at the higher levels of corporate America and in other places. Women are major contributors to the smooth functioning of society. They are important assets to this nation in the truest sense of the word. They are protected by law. Retaliation against women is a serious matter. In all work environments, men and women must work together in peace and unity.

It should be remembered that sexual encounters and love are two different dynamics. One may gain the body—but not necessarily the soul and heart. Sex is often used as a weapon for all sorts of reasons. Even female Russian spies use sex into seducing men. Sex is often used for good and evil reasons. Therefore, please understand these dynamics and govern yourself accordingly.

Sexual harassment charges and allegations against men in corporate America and elsewhere aren't the only trials and tribulation facing this nation. Political strife, crime, violence, opioid addiction, and ignorance are other factors and are working against this nation and its people in a profound way.

Poverty and failing educational institutions in urban and rural areas are other dynamics in the equation. This nation can do better. We better do better before it's too late. The American people are being watched by our allies and adversaries. We cannot afford to let down our allies, and we certainly cannot afford to let down the next generation of Americans. And so the time has arrived for action. We must turn this nation around and move away from the destructive path it's taking and go in the right direction.

The News Media

Have you ever noticed that the news media seems to be fanning the flames of strife in this country? It is not just from a political standpoint; it goes across the spectrum. In terms of political bias, this is clear to everyone. The news media should be fair and impartial, but this is far from what's been the case. People in this profession, if we can refer to them as professionals, show their biases with impunity. It seems as though these people are interested only in reporting bad news instead of good news. The bad reports seem to take precedence over the good news. The worst part is that bad news seems to travel with lightning speed, and the good news is often swept under the carpet. People in the news business aren't reporting objectively. They have their motives, and this is unfortunate.

Executives in the news media claimed that: "the reason black reporters aren't giving public discourse it's because they are ruff around the edges." Is this the reason as they claimed? Where are the black Journalists, Reporters, Hankers, etc? Are we to believe that Africans Americans in the categories mentioned aren't available? And that they are ruff around the edges, and impolite as they proclaimed? You be the Judge.

The divine misfortunes of the descendants of Cain are also a factor in the equation, in terms of the decline facing this nation. Can the curse affecting the generation of Cain be lifted? Can the misfortune be broken? Are the descendants of Cain aware of this fact? If they are, what are they doing about it? The generation of Cain is supposed to be Christian. If this is the case, they should have known the Golden Rule: Ask and you shall receive, seek and you shall find, knock and it shall be open.

Cain and Abel

> *And Cain talked with Abel his brother: and it came to pass, when they were in the field, that Cain rose up against Abel his brother, and slew him. And the Lord said unto Cain, where is Abel thy brother? And he said, I know not: Am I my brother's keeper? And he said, What has thou done? the voice of thy brother's blood crieth unto me from the ground. And now art thou cursed from the earth, which hath open her mouth to received thy brother's blood from thy hand. (Genesis 4:8-10.)*

The stories of Cain and Abel going back to Adam and Eve are stored in a universal memory bank. As a result, retribution is the legacy of the generations of Cain, and others. This has been the case throughout the ages. In fact, slaughtering of brother, by brother, was the result of a Providential curse that was placed on Cain at the beginning of time. Unfortunately, these are some of the trials and tribulations facing this nation and its people today.

Dilemmas Facing the Jews

Let's go back to the beginning of the problems facing the Jewish/Israeli people. Hell broke out in the camp while Moses was on the mountain receiving the Ten Commandments. He was disturbed when he returned to the lower elevation of mount Sinai and saw what the people were doing.

> *When the people saw that Moses was delayed in coming down from the mountain, they gathered around Aaron and said to him, "Come, make us a god who will go before us because this Moses, the man who brought us up out from the land of Egypt, we don't know what happened to him!" (Exodus 32)*
>
> *Then Aaron replied to them, "Take off the gold rings that are on the ears of your wives, your sons, and your daughters ears and bring them to me." So all the people took off the gold rings that were on their ears and brought them to Aaron. (Exodus 32:2.)*
>
> *He took the gold from their hands and, fashioned it with an engraving tool, and made it into an image of a calf. Then they said, "Israel, this is your god, who bought you up from the land of Egypt!" (Exodus 32:4.)*
>
> *When Aaron saw this he built an altar before it; then he made an announcement: "There will*

be a festival to the Lord tomorrow." Early the next morning they arose, offered burnt offerings, and presented fellowship offerings. The people sat down to eat and drink, then got up to revel.(Exodus 32:6.)

The Lord spoke to Moses: "Go down at once! For your people you brought up from the land of Egypt have acted corruptly. They have quickly turned from the way I commanded them;they have made for themselves an image of a calf. They have bowed down to it, sacrificed to it, and said, Israel, this is your God, who brought you up from the land of Egypt. The Lord said to Moses: I have seen this people, and they are indeed a stiff-necked people. Now leave Me alone, so that my anger can burn against them. Then I will make you into a great nation. (Exodus 32:7.)

Now go, lead the people to the place I told you about; see, My angel will go before you. But on the day I settle accounts, I will hold them accountable for their sin. (Exodus 32: 34.)

And the Lord inflicted a plague on the people for what they did with the calf Aaron had made. (Exodus 32: 35)

This biblical account goes back 6000 years ago. Yet, the Israelite/Jews are still affected, in terms of prosecution. It should be noted that time will not erase the evil stored in the archive of the universe. This is evidence in connection with the plight of the Jewish and Israeli people!

There are people who believe it was the Jews that crucified Jesus. And that's the reason they are been being prosecuted to this day. Biblical history doesn't support this proclamation. And so I present the facts of the matter based on the Bible.

Blood Cursed And The Jewish People

Biblical accounts clearly state that it wasn't the Jewish/Israelites that crucified Jesus. To clear this misconception, quotations from the Bible are given below.

> *Pilate asked them, "what should I do then with Jesus, who is called Messiah?" They all answered, "Crucify Him!" Then he said, Why? What has He done wrong? But they kept shouting, "Crucify Him!" all the more. When Pilate saw that he is getting no where, but that a riot was starting instead, he took some water, washed his hands in front of the crowd, and said, "I am innocent of this man's blood. See to it yourselves!" And all the people answered, "Let his blood be on us and our children, and children's children forever!" (Matthews 27)*

The Crucifixion of Christ was 2000 years ago. Nevertheless, what falls out from the event is still reverberating with the Jews to this day. Could this be another dynamic behind the constant prosecution of the Jewish/Israeli people? My God, this blood curse is devastating! I certainly want no part of that.

Destruction can be placed in two categories: destruction brought about by divine misfortune

and misfortune brought about by karmic retribution. The way to lift this curse from the generation of Cain, and others, can be found within the realms of Providence. Until it is lifted, people will continue bringing vengeance upon others and themselves.

This is where people of religious faith come into the equation. People of religious faith should petition the mercy of the Supreme Being in this regard. People of religious faith are duty bound to act. They should request the intervention of Providence instead of turning against those who are in spiritual and moral darkness.

Other elements can be cited in terms of the troubles facing this nation and its people, and we will bring them to light in later chapters.

Everyone who originated in Cain's generation has been affected by Cain's misfortune. It should be clear that misfortune affects different people in different ways. This is dependent upon reason of affluence or poverty, education, and ignorance. A physician, for example, probably wouldn't be tempted to commit an armed robbery. However, he might be tempted into having non-consensual sexual relations with his patient. In fact, this is a problem in this country to this day! This is not to say that the doctor raping his patient is not a crime. On the other side of the spectrum, people at lower levels of society are often tempted by violent criminal activities, including armed robbery and murder. One of the elements that's keeping violence alive is the influence of nefarious forces. These forces are from the realm of darkness.

I firmly believe that nefarious forces are there for a reason. If nefarious forces weren't in existence, curses, misfortunes, and other evil would not prevail in our world. However, people were created with free will. This is the will to do good or evil. These are the forces, unfortunately, that punish people for their sins and wicked deeds.

Providence is able to vanquish the devil and his legions from the earth. Nevertheless, they are there for good reasons. Good and evil must coexist. The choice is up to us as to the one we chose to embrace. We will be rewarded—or we will be punished—based on the choices that we make in life or in the life to come.

The archangels and angels are benevolent messengers of the universe. They are not the legion of demons of the dark domain. Angels do good work, but they are capable of bringing destruction. Lucifer and his legion of evil demons aren't interested in good and benevolent activities. They oppose everything and anything in the universe that is good. They even oppose the Creator and Sustainer of the universe. As for people, you have seen what they have done to them throughout the ages.

They have hardened the hearts of many people and planted discord, hatred, and jealousy within them. Many people bring destruction to other people. These are the ways of life around the earth and in the United States. Evil is on the rise across the globe. People's inhumanity to others is alive and well in this day and age. You are probably aware of the barbarism and brutalities that are taking place in the Middle East and in other places across the globe.

In terms of evil, the angels of darkness have been there since the beginning of time, and they are fanning the flames of evil against people. They are the entities that instigated the deception against Cain to slaughter Abel. They haven't gone anywhere; they are influencing people into nefarious actions all across the globe. People should be aware of the existence of these entities and their abilities to bring ruin through deception and deceitful activities. People with unsavory tempers are prime targets for evil and deceptions. I am cautioning my brothers and sisters to be careful with your action. Remember, an ounce of prevention is better than a pound of cure!

The good news is that people were not placed on earth to wander hopelessly. We were given instructions to combat the power of darkness. This includes the Ten Commandments. Yet, people have failed miserably in this regard. Failing to obey the Commandments has brought additional punishment upon people and the environment. I will bring the Commandments to your attention in chapter 9.

The All-Seeing Eyes

"The eyes of the Lord roam through the universe, beholding the good and evil." You are already aware that the universal eye and ears sees us and hears us. Based on this concept, nothing we do can be hidden. Whatever took place in the dark will come to light; whatever secret was hidden will eventually be revealed. This is clearer today than ever before. Malfeasance in connection with acquisitions brought by women, and others, have been brought to light, and will come to light. Not only in this country, but counties across the globe as well. I intend to point our people in the right direction. This direction will lead to peace, happiness, and prosperity.

Trivialities Vs Morality

Many Americans are pursuing trivial things to such an extent that they have failed miserably in the search for spiritual and divine things. As a result, many people are miserable, unhappy, and uncertain about the future. There are desperate conditions for the mind, body, and the soul. I have the appropriate remedies for these conditions. I will give you the prescription throughout this book.

There is nothing wrong with the pursuit of material things. The accumulation of material possessions is natural. A comfortable home, peaceful environment, and pleasure and happiness are all noble pursuits, but one should balance the pursuit of these things with honesty, integrity, and uprightness. Stealing, killing, engaging in adulterous activities, and bearing false witness against one's neighbor for profit or gain will be at one's own peril. On the other side of the spectrum, one should learn to balance the pursuit of material possessions with spiritual and divine understanding.

The soul will not find peace in material possessions. The soul seeks to be united with its Maker. It is your duty and responsibility to allow this unity to be established.

Help The Less Fortunate

Those who have reached the top in terms of wealth have a duty and responsibility to those at the lower economic levels of society. The rich and famous can assist those in the lower economic levels in many ways. They are able to provide affordable housing, skills training, and motivational assistance to those at the lower economic levels. If you give the world the best you have, the best will come back to you.

Wouldn't it be nice if wealthy American citizens came to the aid and assistance of urban and rural area kids at the lower end of the economic spectrum? Wouldn't it be nice if the rich extended assistance in adhering to the suggestions mentioned above? A little suggestion will go a long way in awakening the conscience, the will, and the desire of wealthy Americans. And so I invite affluent Americans to answer this call. Do all the good you can, and it will come back to you tenfold.

Charity is the mother of mercy. Charity is good for the mind, body, and soul. Those who contribute charitably will have no regrets. I know, the desire to hold tight to whatever we have is strong. Nevertheless, until we are willing and ready to offer assistance to the less fortunate, peace and happiness with our soul may be wishful thinking.

Billionaire Under Fire

A wealthy New York businessman is under fire for running-for-the 2020 presidential election. This candidate has spent almost $400.0000.000 of his own money competing with the rest of the presidential hopefuls. His supporters and admirers are delighted and are cheering this candidate on. Naturally, this has come to the attention of his critics and opponents. They are outraged. They believe that this man has launched an unfair competition for the party's nomination due to his enormous wealth and power. I am not sure as to how these things will eventually play out, but stay tuned.

The following breakdown revealed the areas of spending in connection with politics between 4 to 6 weeks of 2020: According to Advertising Analyst, this wealthy businessman in question, has spent $260 million on broadcast TV, $24 million on cable, $9 million on radio broadcast, and $64 million on digital, for a total of $357 million.

Now, think of the amount of poor kids that could have been helped with the fortune? This case is not an isolated one! These things happen all of the time. In the meantime, ignorance and poverty reign.

If this nation wants to remain a superpower, it must begin educating the masses, instilling moral values, enhancing human relationship, and eradicating poverty and illiteracy. We must give every American a first-class education, including poorer people from urban and rural areas. Our nation is not at the top—or even the middle—in terms of educating our people. This cannot continue; change is necessary.

On the other side of the spectrum, morality seems to be declining. Based on this factor, the use and abuse of opioids and other narcotics is on the rise. If this epidemic is not reversed, what will be the future of the United States? What will happen to the next generation of Americans? Where will the next innovators, engineers, scientists, and technologists come from? America will certainly be lagging far behind—even behind developing nations—and we will have only ourselves to blame.

Human relationships are another major problem. Although some progress has been made, ignorance is still with us. People can do without this depravity. Naturally, the problem of racism is based on ignorance. There are people of different races, cultures, and ethnic backgrounds all over the globe. This was the original intention of the Almighty Creator. Accepting humans for what they are is a product of wisdom, knowledge, and understanding.

This chapter brought to your attention the fundamentals of the workings of the universe. It mentioned the providential misfortune placed on Cain for slaying his brother, Abel, and that it is still affecting people today. Universal eyes are overlooking the universe to dispense rewards or punishments. We give a bird's-eye view of the major planets and their effects on the human race.

Maintaining superpower status demands excellence. We mentioned the necessary steps that must be taken to maintain superpower status.

In the next chapter, I present startling revelation from Divine Providence. I brought to your attention things of a divine and providential nature: tilting of the poles, lowering of the earth's temperature, and the rebirth of the planet earth. Providence announced the faith of our planet and the necessary steps mother nature is taking to correct and preserve our earth. As for people, arrogance, selfishness, and greed haven't gone unnoticed. These things are addressed in the chapter.

CHAPTER 2

Messages from Divine Providence

This revelation of things to come upon the earth was revealed by the angel Gabriel. Providence deemed it necessary to bring to the attention of the inhabitants of this terrestrial domain that which is to come on our planet. I am fortunate to be able to bring this revelation to you. Miracles do happen. This is the case as it relates to the information presented in this chapter. What you are about to read is unusual. Nevertheless, revelations are nothing new. Those of you who are familiar with biblical texts are aware of these things.

Revelations of secrets and mysteries aren't new. Whatever there is to be known in the past were revealed. That which is to be known in the future will be revealed.

Providence will reveal to humanity whatever is deemed necessary. These revelations presented by the angels were intended for you to know. Please don't be alarmed, angels are messengers from your Father in heaven. They (your guardian angels) carry your prayers up to heaven to the Lord.

On the other hand, there are secrets and mysteries that will remain secrets to the human race. I am about to bring things to your attention that were intended to be revealed for the good and welfare of the human race. The universe, the power controlling the universe, God, Providence, or whatever name or title is appropriate for you from a religious point of view is acceptable. In any event, a higher power is at work in the universe. These things were brought to your attention. Yet, they will be more apparent to you when you read these revelations.

This earth is out of balance. Clearly, it appears as though Divine Providence isn't pleased with the conditions of this planet. It is not a coincidence that you are reading this revelation in connection with the shifting of the North and South Poles, the cooling of the earth, and the ice and cooling that is to come. We are all given an opportunity to prepare for the cooling of this planet that is coming. I strongly believe that the process has already started. The unusual weather patterns happening around the globe and in this country are visible to everyone. One doesn't have to be meteorologist to understand the weather patterns across the globe is changing. Young and tender shoots are coming to the surface in January when it's supposed to be the dead of winter in some places. Inconsistent weather patterns are visible to everyone: warm weather one day, cold weather the next day, tornadoes, hurricanes, and volcanic activities. Now you will be aware of the dynamics behind the unusual phenomena.

Some people are slow readers, and others don't read at all. Notwithstanding these differences, they should be aware of the message in this book. My duty is to make these revelations known to everyone. This is a gigantic challenge. How am I going to accomplish this task? With the technology of books on tape, this is possible. There are books on CD or DVD these days. I will mobilize all the will at my disposal to make these revelations known to as many people as possible. Those of you who are able to assist are welcome to do so. Please help me get this book into the hands of as many souls as possible. The angelic revelations transcend religious traditions and beliefs. I am concerned about this planet and its future. I am also concerned about the existence of humans on this planet. The tilting of the poles will affect people and should be of concern to everyone.

I believe that some will scoff at what will be revealed. To them, I say, "You are welcome to do so, but you will do so at your own peril." If a blind person cannot see the sun, that will not prevent the sun from existing. Those with sight see the sun, and blind people don't. The question of whether you believe, or do not believe, has no part in logic. You either know, or don't know. And if you are ignorant of a fact, you should educate yourself of the fact. I hope that I am making myself clear.

There are people who don't believe in spiritual and divine things. To them, I say, "We shouldn't cast pearls before swine. They cannot recognize them; they will trample over them." Please note that I meant no disrespect to you, nor am I referring to you as swines. Just an analogy! There are people who only believe in things they can see and touch. Do they believe in God? They cannot see or touch God, the element of air, or the foundation of the earth.

Without any further commentary, please let me bring to your attention the revelations given in connection with changes that are coming in to our world.

Part I: Archangel Gabriel and Mother Mary

Archangel Gabriel

> "I come with greetings of great joy just as I did two thousand years ago and just as I have done many times since. My greetings of joy are needed by you and your planet now. Two thousand years ago, the birth of Christ, an energy, showed and taught you unconditional love. Now with the arrival of advent, we once again welcome back that beautiful energy of the ascended Christ to be with us and to bring us peace. This time, he wishes his energy to arrive and be reborn upon this planet for all, devoid of institution, structure, dogma or hierarchy. The ascended Christ is here now for all of you—young or old or rich or poor—wherever you are around the world. He is not separate from other beings that you already know and love."

Mother Mary

"He works with all of the assented masters and all of the archangels. As his divine mother, it is my duty here to rebirth him. Gabriel and I, Mary, are so intertwined this month that we speak with one voice—you will find it hard to separate us. We understand, from a human perspective, that it is easier if we allow that separation. But truly, the merging right now of these two energies of Mary and of Gabriel, who is also here right now, is what happens all the time in the spiritual realm. We do not see ourselves as separate from each other, you see. That is a human construct that you have created to help yourself understand, and in particular, for the mind to understand. The new teaching will come from the heart as was always intended, and within the heart space, many can dwell at the same time."

End of Part I

Part II Message For The People Of The Earth

Archangel Gabriel

"A lowering of temperature, particularly in the Northern Hemisphere, but not just there. Snow may fall in unexpected places, and we are not to fear. That is part of the earth, part of Gaia's natural cycle, of balance and correction. But with both of these energies, purification comes also."

(Note, Gabriel is talking about a lowering of temperature in the Northern Hemisphere—but not just there. This lowering of the temperature will correct the ecosystem. It's true, the ecosystem is completely out of balance. Remember, those young shoots I brought to your attention, are springing up in January, which is supposed to be winter here in the United States.)

Gabriel

> "You are to look after those in your community who need looking after, especially the old, the poor, and the elderly. Make sure those in your community are cared for during the ice and cold. This message is given so you can prepare for the cold and ice that will come. The coldness and ice have to do with preserving what will still be needed in the new age, but when the ice melts, some structural material will have decayed and rotted from the waters. That which survives was meant to survive. This is actually symbolic of what needs to happen for the earth to rebirth itself.

The elements of air and water are going to teach us a lot. They are going to demonstrate a lot. We should be observant and tune in to them. You cannot fight nature. You cannot fight what is coming. You need to work with them.

Glaciers are going to melt. The polar bears are in trouble. We have held off these changes on our planet for centuries in the hope that humanity would change its ways, but so many people are still stuck in their old ways and do not want to let go of old worn structural beliefs. Change has to come in, and water is the element that will bring in this change. Change has to come in for the new life on this planet to evolve.

When the ice melts, it is going to reveal some amazing things that have never been seen on this planet. Places of beauty will be revealed. Great portals will be revealed that we never knew existed. There will be a gradual shifting of the poles instead of a radical shifting. A radical shifting of the poles would be too dramatic, and it would take too long for it to be recover from. The council decreed that a radical change would be too traumatic.

Humans will survive. There is no threat to people's survival. However, there may be a correction of the unbalance that exists on the earth; overpopulation, deforestation, plundering of the seas, pollution of the air, desecration of the land cannot be allowed to continue.

We are on a path, which if nature doesn't step in to correct, we have the power, on a human level, to destroy the earth to a point where it will become inhabitable. What Mother Nature seeks to do in the gentlest way possible is bring about corrections to balance the many systems on this planet. And it will be done for the good of all.

It will be done for the highest good of every system on this planet. The animals, plants, and vegetation—every single system—will be treated equally, with care and compassion for the good of all.

People have gotten out of control. There needs to be regulation of the kindest, gentlest ways possible.

Don't go into fear. We will reveal more when the time is right. This is more a message to prepare, and that doesn't mean stockpiling, hoarding, or panicking. It means going into the deepest place of faith and trust. Do you trust us to deliver a more peaceful pure world for all—or do you not? We hope you trust us because we have the highest intentions for all beings to be respected and loved. All of this is written in a soul contract; there are no surprises.

This rebalancing needs to be done, and it will be done. That should not be surprising. We will say more about this when the time is right.

Look after each other. Don't think of your own needs. Think of your neighbor—and realize that you been given spiritual tools and light to keep you safe.

There is much that you can do to keep yourself and your community safe. You are being asked to balance your own life. Why would Gaia not do the same thing? Gaia is a living, breathing being—just as you are. Anything that is to be corrected will be corrected. Those who wish to carry on the journey with her can do so, but there has to be an opening of hearts and coming together.

Regarding the behavior of your fellow humanity, a humbleness, a beauty needs to come in to cover the arrogance and greed, and it will be so. It will happen through the elements. The elements are there to serve us—they don't wish to harm us—but there will be correction to the planet. We will be with you every step of the way. There is nothing to fear."

To the skeptic, are you still not believing in things spiritual and divine? The archangel Gabriel brings attention to the fact that the elements are there to help us and not to hurt us. The question is, what are these elements? Let's look at what constitute the elements.

The Elements

There are four elements: air (wind), earth (Gaia), water, and fire. These elements are dangerous in their own ways. Everyone is aware of the destructive nature of fire, especially when it is out of control. Many people have died in buildings and automotive-related fires. Volcanoes are fire, even lightning falls under the category of fire, and they are all dangerous.

The element of water is no less dangerous. The sinking of the *Titanic* in 1912, and other vessels since then, and the lives that were lost are testament to the destructive nature of water. Rivers, lakes, and streams are all elements of water. They can be deadly. Many lives have been lost over the years due to floods.

This brings us to the element of earth. Earthquakes, landslides, collapsed caves, and mines are all dangerous motions of Gaia, the element of earth. Many people have lost their lives in earthquakes. Collapsed caves and mines have claimed many lives over the years.

Finally, there is the element of air or wind. Air is by far the most dangerous of them all, in my opinion. Tornadoes, hurricanes, and windstorms are all works of the element of the winds.

There you are. Mother Nature is good, but she can hurt us. These elements are good for the most part, but they can be dangerous as well.

We hope that your eyes have been opened to wisdom and truth in connection to the elements and the duties they perform.

Since we are on this subject, have you considered the awesome wonders of the sea?

The Mighty Oceans and the Seas

Since the beginning of time, all the rivers, streams, and lakes of the earth have flowed into the seas, yet they never overflow their boundaries. Have you ever considered the reason behind this secret or mystery? To answer this question, I will turn to the book of Job.

The Story of Job

According to the Bible, Job was a righteous, God-fearing man, and he found favor with the Lord. The Lord tested Job's sincerity by placing grave afflictions upon him. During his afflictions, Job never disavowed or disparaged the Lord—even when his wife told him that he should curse God and die. Job told his wife that she is a foolish woman, and rightfully so!

Instead, Job questioned his reason for living and the pain and suffering he endured. He cursed the day he was born. According to the text, the Lord answered Job from a whirlwind:

> *Who is this who obscure my council with ignorant words? (Job 38)*
>
> *Get ready to answer me like a man; when I question you, you will inform Me. (Job 38:2)*
>
> *Where were you when I established the earth? Tell Me, if you have understanding. (Job 38:4)*
>
> *Who fixed its dimension? Certainly you know. (Job 38:5)*
>
> *What supports its foundations? (38:6)*

> *Who laid its cornerstone while the morning stars sang together and all the sons of God shouted for joy? (Job 38:7).*
>
> *Who enclosed the sea behind doors when it burst from the womb, when I made the clouds its garment and thick darkness its blanket, when I determined its boundaries and put its bars and doors in place, when I declared: You may come this far; but no farther; your proud waves stop here? (38:8–11)*
>
> *Job was spooked, he was afraid. He apologized. Then job replied to the Lord: "I know that you can do anything and no plan of Yours can be thwarted." You asked, "Who is this who conceals My counsel with ignorance?" Surely I spoke about things I did not understand, things too wonderful for me to know. You said, "Listen now, and I will speak. When I question you, you will inform Me." I had heard rumors about You, but now my eyes have seen You. Therefore I take back my words and repent in dust and ashes." (Job 42:2–6)*

There you are. These are some of the things I contemplate. They keep me up at might—and so should you.

Based on divine revelation, I firmly believe that the sea will never overstep its appointed boundary—no matter what scientists are trying to tell you. However, if it is the Lord's will to bring destruction on the earth by way of the sea, people will be powerless against doing anything about it.

The angel Gabriel is a messenger who was entrusted to deliver several important messages on God's behalf. Gabriel appeared to at least three people according to the Bible: first to the prophet Daniel; next to the priest Zechariah to foretell and announce the birth of John the Baptist; and finally to the Virgin Mary to tell her that she would conceive and bear a son. Gabriel is the angel of annunciation. He is the one who revealed that the Savior was to be called Jesus.

I sincerely hope that you do understand that the Virgin Mary and the archangel Gabriel delivered these revelations from the Lord. I am placing the emphasis here on people's arrogance and greed. I believe injustice, crime, hatred, and violence have not gone unnoticed by the powers governing the universe.

People have gotten out of control. Deceptions, wicked deeds, lack of concern for others, and all sorts of evil schemes are embarrassments to the Creator of the universe. It is no wonder that the Lord grieved that he had made people.

Providential Regret

> *"When the Lord saw that people's wickedness was widespread on the earth and that every scheme is mind thought of was nothing but evil all the time, the Lord regretted that He had made people on the earth, and He was grieved in His heart. Then the Lord said, I will wipe off the face of the earth: people, whom I created, together with the animals, creatures that crawl, and birds of the skies—for I regret that I made them. (Genesis 6:5–7)*
> *Noah found favor in the eyes of the Lord. (Genesis 6:8)*

Things on the earth have not changed since the days of Noah, have they? Regrettably, things have worsened many times since then. There is no sign indicating that there will be any changes in the immediate or foreseeable future.

The Lord grieved He had made people. He kept His promise and brought a deluge and wiped the earth clean of every living thing. Noah, his family, and other things that were on the ark were saved. Let's wait in joyful hope for that which is to come on this planet we call earth.

The question of overpopulation of the earth is something to think about. Deforestation of the land, plundering of the seas, and pollution of the air are of concern to Providence. We are being watched by the universe or some superior entity up there. The good and the evil things are being recorded. I brought these things to your attention in previous chapters.

As for humanity, greed, arrogance, and selfishness were cited by providential revelation. Selfishness and greed are some of humanity's worst depravities.

Notwithstanding the pervasive poverty in Africa, the Middle East, and elsewhere, a Saudi prince recently purchased a painting for more than $400 million. This is only one example of selfishness. In the United States, these things take place constantly. There are those who go without. There are children and adults who have little or no food. There are people in this country without places to rest their heads, yet there are the wealthy people who are living in million-dollar mansions and driving luxury cars while their less fortunate brothers and sisters are in need. Do these people have hearts? You be the judge of that.

How could a loving God not regret the actions of these people? How could the powers oversee the functioning of the universe not be disgusted by these injustices? How about hatred among humanity, the taking of innocent lives, the pain that has been inflicted by others unjustly? We thank the Lord that changes are coming. You have been told about the changes that are coming. We will be fortunate if this rebalancing of the earth doesn't result in another deluge like in the days of Noah.

What follows will be shocking to many. Below, you will find relevant information that's unique. I leave it to your imagination to determine what entity or deity would make such comments from the spiritual realm.

This world is truly mysterious, isn't it? The longer we live, the more we learn. Learning is a lifelong process that we brought to your attention in earlier chapters. The following observations and revelations were given at the conclusion of part I and part II. I would like this to be separate and distinct from the above. I would like you to think carefully about the comments below. Who would make such a revelation? What deity, being, or entity would make such a profound revelation? I leave it to your imagination. You be the judge. In any event, whenever you make up your mind, you may want to send up a little prayer to the universe. You are now aware of the fact that the universe has a mind, eyes, ears, and a memory.

Part III Christ speaks

> *"With great love, you have 2000 years to bring in this love that I talked of. And yet we do not judge you. This love didn't happen by the majority of*

people on your planet. But this needs to happen. And we been very patience with you. We will be with you until the end of time. Note, this revelation was presented by the master Jesus. This being that Mother Mary mentioned above. This said Jesus who suffered under Pontius Pilate; was crucified, dead and buried: He descended into hell, the third day he arose again from the dead: He ascended into heaven, and sits on the right hand of God the Father Almighty. From thence He shall come to judge the quick and the dead."

Christians and Jews shouldn't have any difficulty deciphering and understanding the above quote. Christ teaches His disciples, and others, brotherly love, kindness, peace, and goodwill among other things. To this day, there is no peace on earth or goodwill to others, from others, for the majority of the earth. Lord, please have mercy on the human race.

There is an inevitability of what is to come. What is it going to take to wake up humanity on this planet? There is more to life than meets the eye. There's more to things than some have ever seen or comprehended. Humans aren't permitted to see things that are taking place in the ether. If the veil was removed from our eyes, we would see wondrous things up there.

We are waiting in joyful hope for the changes that are coming on this terrestrial domain. I believe the changes are already taking place across the planet. Have you noticed the weather pattern in the last four to seven years? Many people do, and I hope that you do too.

Is There Life Beyond the Grave?

It depends on what death means in the first place. Yes, the soul survives death, and I am going to prove this to you. About six months or so after my father was dead and buried, his soul, or spirit, appeared to me from beyond the grave in a dream. My father appeared to me in the family's backyard just as he always did in his life when he was using the barbecue grill. He loved corn and would always barbecue corn on the cob on our back porch. In this dream, I found myself going to the back porch. When I went there, my father was barbecuing in his usual pants, shirt, and shoes. I approached him and said, "What is happening, Dad?"

He replied, "Nothing, son. Everything is all right. Wherever they left me, that's where I am. You must help your mother. You must remember to help your mother, son."

I awoke from my dream in astonishment. *Where did they leave my father's remains? Yes, in the cemetery—six feet down under.*

There is all sort of speculations as to whether or not the human soul goes to heaven after it departs the body. Many believe that the soul goes to heaven. Is it true that the soul goes to heaven? The Holy Book tells us the soul returns to God after the body is death. It doesn't mention anything about heaven. The speculation continues.

How much do you know about angels/guardian angels? Many people do, many don't. For those of you who do not, I am going to prove it to you that you are wrong, dead wrong! You do have a guardian angel.

Guardian Angels

The moment that you were born into this life you were assigned at least one guardian angel. The angel will be with you for the duration of your life here on this earth. A guardian angel's duty and responsibility is overseeing your welfare, your destiny, if you will. However, your protecting angel will not intervene in your affairs unless you request their help and assistance! It's a question of free will, *your* free will.

Many people are defeated in life due to lack of this knowledge. And so, the information presented below are for your information. You should make an effort to understand, and consciously connect with your guardian angel. I am giving you 3 examples of guardians angels names, based on birth Month and Dates.

I. If you were born between January 1st and 5th the name of your guardian angel is Nemamiah. His Supervising Angel is Mikael. Everyone in the Jewish and Christian communities knows that Archangel Mikael is a great protecting Angel! The angel which fought and defeated Lucifer, the Devil, and his legions of demonic spirits.

II. If you were born between July 28th and August 1st your guardian angel is Maaiah. His Supervising Angel is Hesediel.

III. If you were born between December 3rd and 7th your guardian angel is Hahasiah. His Supervising Angel is Haniel.

Who Are The Angels?

1. Holy Living Creature
2. Wheels
3. Throne
4. Brilliant Ones
5. Fiery Ones
6. Kings
7. Gods
8. Sons of the Elohim
9. Cherubim

Angels are intermediary beings from your father which is in Heaven, the Almighty. Many religions — Judaism Christianity, Islam, and others — recolonized angels and the role they play in the scheme of things. They are, in effect, envoys, messengers, or ambassadors, and are used to designate the angel of Yahweh, or all angelic beings that are part of the court, or council of the Supreme Being.

Angelic Hierarchy

As mentioned earlier, the angelic world is organized according to three perfect hierarchies as follows:

The first hierarchy, the highest order, is made up of Seraphin, Cherubim,and Thrones. They are the closes to the supreme Being. (God) They receive his will over us directly from Him,which they communicate to the inferior hierarchic. They are synonymous to the ministers of the King in human society.

The second hierarchy is made up of the Domination, Quality and Powers. They see that Divine will applied to humans. They are cinemas to the leaders of the King's Army.

The third heirarchy are of the inferior order of angels. They carry out God's command, as far as human beings are concerns. It is because of their inferior nature that they can be so close to human beings. This hierarchy is made up of angels of the order of the Principality. They are in charge of humans' destiny. They range from the order of the Angel-Archangel who announce great news. Finally, to the Angel-Angels, or Guardian Angels, some of whom are your own guardian angel!

How to Call Upon Your Guardian Angel?

By his name and his prayer. If you do not know his name and his prayer, you can still call your protecting angel. I will reveal this to you in a moment. But first, you should know that angels love music, any kind of music. They also love sweet smelling fragrance! They also appreciate when you thank them for their intervention in your affairs.

Now, you can make a request at any time: while driving, walking, sitting in the park, etc. However, for the sake of formality, let me walk you through an effective way to contract your protecting angel in the comfort of your home.

This can be done anytime, However, it is preferable in the evening before going to sleep. This is also very effective when carried out on your birthday.

    I.   Light a white candle, place it in a fireproof container to set a mediating mood. You may put the candle and incense on any solid object: dresser, night stand, coffee table, etc.
    II.   Burn some sweet smelling incense, and play a beautiful selection of music. These are options, however, you want the nicest and most pleasant environment, I believe.
    III.   After the above, call the name of the angel and simply make your request. You may make any request as long as it's in the realm of possibility. Then thank the angel for coming and accepting your petition/request.
    IV.   blow out the candle and you are finished!

Now, if you do not know the name of your guardian angel, simply recite the following prayer after carrying out step I, II, III:

> *"Angel of God, my guardian dear, to whom God's love commits me here, ever this day be at my side, to light and guard, to rule and guide." Amen.*

Then, make your request. You will not see or hear the angel, but he will be there! You can now blow out the candle.

> *For He will give His angels orders concerning you, to protect you, to protect you in all yours ways. (Psalm 91:11)*
>
>   *Don't neglect to show hospitality, for by doing this some welcomed angels as gust without knowing it. Hebrews 13:2)*

Note, in all you undertaking, keep God and Nature's gods on your side to ensure prosperity, success,and good luck! As mentioned, you can call your guardian angel to assist you at any time. Remember, angels are messengers from the Lord! Seek and you will find. You can find addition information in connection with angels in the Libraries, Bookstores, or even searching the World Wide Web. Good luck.

The Power of Spoken Words

The tongue is a powerful instrument. It can dispense blessings, or a curse. As a result, life and death is in the tongue! Be careful not to use disparaging words, curse words, and words of ill will to children and others. I often overhear parents using condemning words to their children without thinking of the consequences: "you will never come to anything, you are too stupid, you will never have anything, you will always be a loser." Unfortunately, these cursed words will manifest themselves in the lives of the accursed. And so, if you do not have words of blessing to give, it would be better to say nothing. Give blessings, not curses.

Past Lives, Future Life

Souls are indestructible! When the body is laid to rest the soul continues on. According to the will of the Creator, souls return based on the laws of reincarnation. The question is, whose responsibility is it to teach these secrets and mystery? Many Protestant Churches teaches about the "Holy spirits, angels of the Lord, spirits of the Lord." They mentioned nothing in connection with the afterlife.

The Roman Catholic Church, on the other hand, goes a little further. Roman Catholics pray for the souls of the departed. This is understandable since souls may be in purgatory (a state of expiation). However, this is as far as the Hierarchy of the Catholic Church will teach the layman.

The truth is, many of us don't know what we were, or what we were doing in past lives: what country we were living in, what race we were, were we male, or were we female, etc. We don't know what we will become in the life after this one. Will you return a wealthy and influential person, or a poor and destitute person?

And so, my advice to my reader, and others, is they should live a life that's above reproach. Be honest and upright in all deportment. Above all, venerate your Almighty Maker. And finally, do good to others as you would have them do unto you.

This chapter brought startling revelations from divine providence to your attention. The condition of Mother Earth was revealed: overpopulation of the earth, plundering of the sea, pollution of the air, etc. The steps necessary for equilibrium restoration were presented. Greed and arrogance that are taking place by our fellowmen were cited by providence. The role of the angels, including your guardian angel and how to contact yours, were brought to your attention. What were you in past life, the one prior to this one? That's the question.

The next chapter will discuss, among other things, the declining United States, and the rising Republic of China. The chapter brings to light detrimental issues that's preventing this nation from remaining at the summit of its greatness.

CHAPTER 3

Declining United States, the Rising China.

We discussed the fundamental aspects of the universe in previous chapters. You are now aware of the fact that the universe isn't static by any stretch of the imagination. Instead, the universe is very dynamic in the truest sense of the word. As a result of this dynamism, the actions and reactions of people are recorded and stored in the memory of the universe. This simply means that the day of reckoning for people will arrive sooner or later. This applied not only to people, but also to nations as well.

The United States seems to have reacted its peak. Reaching the peak of wealth, prestige, and power, and remaining at the peak is another matter. There is much internal strife within the United States that is contributing to destabilization. One of the elements contributing to destabilization originates from the seat of power. This is trickling down massively on both sides of the political spectrum from coast to coast. As a civilized nation, we can do better. Those who are undone with authority to rule this nation should set the example of civility. I will not go into specifics and elaborate on the conduct of one political party as opposed to the conduct of the other. Nevertheless, hatred, bitterness, disdain, and retribution between the major political parties are cause for concern!

And so, America has reached its peak of greatness and failed to remain there. As such, it's descending. Thus, the declining of the United States and its people.

The Nation of China

On the other hand, the nation of China is rising. They are lifting their people out of poverty, ignorance, and despair. They are also doing good deeds by helping Africa to rise. They are investing in infrastructure, housing, farming, the list goes on. They should be commended. They should be commended for reaching out and lending a helping hand to the people on the Continent of Africa.

Europe and America

Notwithstanding the benefits Europe and the United States derived from Africa, they failed to assist in meaningful ways, in terms of development. It is said that the above-mentioned exploit Africa of its natural resources without contributing to the good and welfare of the Continent. And so, if it's the will of the powers controlling the universe that China should rise and dominate, so be it.

People, or nations will receive their just rewards or hellish punishments for their good deeds and their evil deeds. Ignorance of the workings of the universe is no excuse. People should seek knowledge. Humans are duty-bound to seek wisdom, understanding, and knowledge of spiritual and divine things. Everyone has a body, a soul that dwells in that body, and a mind. People generally associate the mind with the brain, but the mind is not the brain. In general, the mind instructs the brain. The mind is complicated. It survives our passing from this physical life (death). To put things in their proper perspective, we say that the mind and the soul survive the death of the body. The soul and the mind continue on after the body dies.

I am bringing these things to your attention for a good reason. I will reveal them soon. First of all, you should understand that your body is not you. You are living in your body just as your body is living in your house. Wisdom dictates that people should think before acting or engaging in things that will be to their detriment or the detriment of others. We should be in tune with the Creator and Sustainer of the universe.

Now that these things are clear to you, let's bring to your attention another element that's contributing to the declining of the nation and its people. One of the first things we should take into consideration is opioid and other narcotics abuse here in the United States. Our people, or many people, are being dumbed down by narcotics. Unfortunately, our government seems to be helpless in these regards.

Drug abuse goes to the core of this nation's troubles. Until drug use and abuse is addressed, corrected, and prevented, there is no telling what the future of America will be. Narcotics abuse is no longer an inner-city epidemic. The curse of drug addiction is in suburban, wealthy, and affluent communities as well. Even if the government was able to prevent illegal narcotics from entering this country, that would not resolve the issue of illegal drugs on the streets. Why is this? Drug-manufacturing facilities are springing up all across this nation. Meth labs can be found all over. If these things are allowed to continue and the war on illegal substance abuse is not won, we will all go down with the sinking ship.

The Opioid Dilemma

The war on opioid abuse is raging. The president of the United Sates has declared a state of emergency. It's not clear to me what the president wanted to accomplish by declaring that state of emergency. Could it stop narcotics users, manufacturers, and suppliers? That would be a step in the right direction, but it will not solve the overall issue of narcotic use in America. Only educated minds can do that. Education can only do so much. There are people who desperately want to go out, and excessive amounts of opioids will terminate their lives.

Whatever the case may be, we are still waiting for the war on opioids to end and victory declared. This crisis has reached epic proportions, and the future isn't looking very good. Many states have legalized the use of marijuana, and many others are contemplating legalization.

In fact, the war on drugs isn't new. It has been raging for decades. As far as we are aware, victory is nowhere in sight. The dumbing down of America is coming from far and wide. It will not be necessary for me to bring to your attention to where these dangerous narcotics are coming from. If the brains of our people are destroyed, then the nation will be destroyed. The destruction of our nation is in progress. I hope I am making this information very clear to you.

The United States has reached the peak of its success and power. However, it's failed to remain at the summit of its success and it's descending. There are many contributing elements and opioid is one of them. The rate of the declining process is questionable. There are people who believe that it's not noticeable, others believe it's gradual, while other proclaimed that it's accelerating. Whatever the case may be there can be no denial that the United States is indeed declining.

The United States is a relative young nation in terms of European American culture, less than 400 years old. This is a short period of time in comparison to other nations and cultures. Will this nation be able to return to the summit and remain there?

In terms of opioids, this brings us to the question of cause and effect, and supply and demand. Unless we remove these dynamics, it's hopeless. The dependency factors should be treated first. Until the need is eliminated, the supply will be in constant demand. This is a vicious cycle, and there is no end in sight.

In the meantime, many people have fallen victim to narcotics abuse, including young adults, mothers, and fathers. Narcotics producers and traffickers are aware of the demand for their products. If the demand didn't exist, the producers and distributors work would all be in vain. It's a vicious circle. Supply and demand are the dynamics at work. We will go to the roots of this evil in a moment.

First, you should understand that many of those who are under the curse of the drug epidemic truly cannot help themselves. Many are under the influence of spiritual strongholds that have been brought about by nefarious or evil demons.

Spiritual strongholds on those caught in the habit are a fact of life. In some cultures, the penalty for addiction is death. Both those who are trafficking and using illegal narcotics are often put to death. This is the wrong approach to this dilemma. The appropriate approach to this phenomenon is expelling the demon by exorcising the evil demon from the victim. The exorcism will take care of the dilemma.

Addiction Is Spiritual Oppression

> *For our battle is not against flesh and blood, but against the rulers, against the authority, against the world powers of this darkness, against the spiritual forces of evil in the heavens. (Ephesian 6:12)*

Evil powers have been working against people since Adam and Eve. Those evil powers deceived Adam and Eve and brought sin, destruction, and death to the human race. These powers are still with us today. Demons can and often do possess people. These things been happening since biblical times. Christians are aware that Christ preformed exorcisms when he drove demons out of young people.

Exorcism

In the biblical story, a demon-possessed young man was plagued by evil spirits night and day. This man lived beside a cemetery. As a result, he was tormented by evil spirits. This man was vexed by these powers from hell, and no one ever dared to confront him. He could not be approached and often inflicted harm on himself and others.

Jesus was passing by, and the boy's father asked him to have mercy on his demon-possessed son. Jesus agreed and commanded the demons to come out of the boy. The head evil spirit requested that Jesus allow them to enter into the head of the swine that were in close proximity. After the demons left the boy, they entered the swine. The boy returned to his senses immediately.

After entering the bodies of the swine, the spirits became confused. They chased each other off a cliff and drowned in a lake.

This was the first recorded exorcism, and it was performed by Jesus, the Messiah.

Could this be the reason why some religions forbid their members from consuming pork and pork products? One never knows. There are people who will never touch anything that is connected with pork or pork products. This has to do with their religious beliefs.

In terms of evil spirits, there are people who are specialists in driving out demons. Christ gave his followers power over demons:

Summoning His twelve disciples, He gave them authority over unclean spirits, to drive them out and to heal every disease and sickness. (Matthew 10)

There are people who are commissioned by Providence to do these things today. Every problem has a solution, and this should never be forgotten.

Let's continue our story in connection with demon-possessed people. Everyone in that community was aware of the demon-possessed man. Being freed of the evil spirits, he returned to his community. Those who knew of him and his issues were astonished and amazed to see that he had been freed from the evil spirits and had returned to normalcy. They questioned him. They wanted to know what had happened to him. He broke the news and told his neighbors that Jesus had intervened and cured him. That was the first exorcism. Had he not been freed from the demons, there is no telling what he would have done to others or himself. The moral of the story is that people are often possessed by demons.

Much of the savagery carried out in the Middle East and elsewhere is carried out by demon-possessed people. They are often vexed by Satan and his evil demons. They will bring vengeance on everyone and anyone in their paths. ISIS and the Taliban are full of evil spirits. Unfortunately, there are demon-possessed people in this country as well.

It should be clear to everyone that there are many gods. However, we are making reference to the Supreme God—that God that Christians, Jewish, and people of other religions believe in. The God who revealed himself to Moses. The Almighty that gave people the Ten Commandments. God is benevolent—all good—but he is capable of bringing vengeance on people. One of the commandments forbids the taking of the life of others. God forbid his people from bringing harm to others. God declared, "Vengeance belongs to me. I will repay them."

Malevolent gods permit the slaughtering of others. Those gods permit the taking of innocent lives. You have seen these things taking place in other countries—to the dismay of people who believe in and worship the God of Moses. We are witnessing evil being playing out in the Middle East and in the West. Those who slaughtered in the name of god, even the innocents, I wondered which of them they are referring to.

Slaughtering in the name of religion, which is proclaimed by some religious fanatics, is forbidden by providential doctrine. Biblical doctrine doesn't support that sort of thing. Unfortunately, this savagery has reached the West and American society. These things, including taking innocent lives, are taking place in our country. Some of the atrocities are carried out by home-grown savages, and others are carried out by savages from abroad who are residing in America. Wherever these demon-possessed people go, they take their curses along with them.

As long as there is evil, atrocities will be carried out by demon-possessed people. I raise these issues to make an important point: people can be possessed by demons. You may have heard the expression about beating the devil out of someone. Many people may not realize the deep meaning behind the statement, which is that the person is possessed and needs an exorcism.

I say all of the above to make an important point. Addiction to opioids or other narcotics can be related to strongholds, issues, or demonic possession. If this is the case, curing the disease entails getting to the root of the problem. A halfway house will yield zero results if the addiction has been brought about by the curse of a stronghold dynamic possession.

Many addicts are aware that their lives could end while taking LSD, doing crack, or taking opioids, yet they go ahead with the destructive process. They cannot resist the temptation. Alas, many people have lost their lives during the process.

The average person has no power over spiritual strongholds. One of the cures is to consult with a stronghold professional. A spiritualist can evaluate the situation when a loved one is under the influence of a narcotics addiction. There are many stronghold specialists out there. Seek—and you will find. The best cure is resisting the urge to consume illegal narcotics. An ounce of prevention is worth a pound of cures.

Many dire situations are facing this nation and its people. It would seem as though the destruction of the brains of the present generation and the next generation of Americans is what is at stake here. We could do without the problem of mind alteration of our people. This nation is currently in need of brilliant minds, and we have a duty and responsibility to keep the masses free from mind-altering substances.

Illegal narcotics are invading our schools. We must take a stand against destroying the minds and lives of young people. Otherwise, we will become the laughing stock of developed and developing nations. How can we declare victory in this war on drugs? It will not be easy. Nevertheless, awareness would be a good place to start. This means that staying away from all forms of opioids and other narcotics should be an integral part of teaching in our educational institutions.

We may have lost this generation to the dynamic of drug addiction, but we should do whatever is necessary to save the next ones. Saving the next generation of Americans should be given priority over everything else.

It's unfortunate that the production of illegal drugs occurs throughout the country. Marijuana is legal in many states these days, and marijuana clinics are all over the place. Getting illegal substances out of the hands of Americans seems like a lost cause.

Fortunately, not everyone has the desire to get high on illegal substances. This is currently the saving grace for this nation. There are Americans who stay away from all illegal substances. I am one of them. Many of us don't do drugs and will not do drugs under any circumstances. To these people, I say more power to them. May they bring inspiration to those who are on the wrong path in terms of destruction to themselves, their loved ones, and their nation.

We can rise above this dependency on a quick fix using mind-altering substances. We look forward to that day when a majority of Americans follows in this direction of avoiding illegal substances and marijuana.

There is a question of wealth versus poverty in America. Have you ever considered the plight of those who are in poverty in the wealthiest nation on earth? Poverty is an unfortunate problem in the United States.

Poverty in America

Poverty in America is a cause for concern for everyone in this country. People in other nations might question the authenticity of this statement when America is supposed to be the wealthiest nation in the world. The poor will always be with us, but poverty should be alien in the United States. What's the reason behind the poverty in this country? It should have been eradicated long ago. Poverty has no place in America.

Why does poverty exist in such a powerful nation? The American people should be contemplating this question. There are many reasons why poverty exists in the United States, and we will look into them. Before we continue, you should understand that if there is no vision, the people will be sure to perish. This is the main factor behind the dilemma of poverty.

One of the problems in this country as it relates to poverty and hopelessness is related to a lack of foresight or vision. The dynamics behind poverty have far-reaching implications. I intend to bring motivational assistance to the masses, which will enable them to prepare themselves for the future. This nation is in need of skilled workers, and there are young Americans without marketable skills. How can these things be? Who are we to blame for this? There is plenty of blame to go around.

Fortunately, people in this country have the opportunity to lift themselves out of poverty—if they repair themselves. This brings us to another question. Why are there so many opportunities and so much poverty? Those at the poverty line have good opportunities to lift themselves out of their dilemmas, but why aren't they moving from poverty to affluence? It is a lack of vision. Preparing for the future seems to be alien to some people. As a result, many people are miserable. They lack an adequate education, marketable skills, and the will to lift themselves up by the bootstraps. Those in lower economic levels could produce food to feed the nation, themselves, and other nations. Farming may not be attractive to some people, but it is an honorable endeavor.

The world needs food. The United States has the resources to grow food to feed the world and its people. If we could produce food for people in other nations, we would make a ton of money. Those at the poverty line would generate enormous wealth by growing and marketing food.

Why aren't we making the desert bloom? Americans should be able to take care of our own people who are in need before lending a helping hand to foreign nations. There are kids going without food, clothes, and shelter right in this country. These deficiencies don't reflect our superpower status.

In terms of producing food, we have the machinery, the technology, and the manpower. One thing that is lacking is the will. Able-bodied men and women who are poor can invest in producing agricultural products. Government should take the lead in organizing such an undertaking. Those at the lower end of the economic spectrum should be given the resources to lift themselves out of poverty and despair.

These are some of the things that the government should be introducing to people who want to lift themselves out of poverty. These are some of the things the government should be doing rather than investing in going to other planets. The enormous amount of resources that the government is using to prepare people to travel to Mars and Jupiter should be used to improve the lives of impoverished Americans. Can fish live on dry land? Will people be able to survive on distant planets? Our bodies weren't conditioned to occupy other planets.

The Creator made people to dwell on earth. Venturing to distant planets was not the divine plan. There will be nothing to gain from venturing to other planets. Let's put our money where our mouths are. Let's use the American taxpayers' money to benefit the lives of those who are in need—right in this country. Until we do that, poverty will continue to plague this nation and its people.

Meanwhile, due to poverty, ignorance, and hopelessness, robberies and other deplorable activities are out of control. Frankly, these and other dilemmas are snares on the reputation of our nation and its people. These things cannot be tolerated. We must lift those at the bottom up. The time to begin the process is now. We are duty bound to lift up those who have fallen and those who are falling.

It's disgraceful that there are children who go without food. Unless we turn these things around, people in this country will continue to live in fear—and rightfully so.

Hungry people are angry people. We have sympathy for those who cannot find food, pay the rent, or provide the necessities for their families and themselves. Many of these people find it necessary to engage in robbery, stealing, or taking the lives of others. These actions aren't appropriate ways to resolve these issues. Those who are involved in these sorts of things will surely bring providential misfortune on themselves. Providential retribution will be brought on the offenders, and the offenders will end up behind bars for criminal activities.

Citizens of developed nations should be educated. There should be no place for ignorance in such a society—and certainly not in the United States of America. Let's look into the educational system in this country.

Education

The masses are supposed to be naive, according to the ruling class. They also believe that they don't need information. If this is the case, then we aren't doing a good job educating the American masses.

There's reason to believe that people in urban and rural areas aren't receiving first-class educations as they should. Education is a great light. Those who had been denied this light will be in darkness from an intellectual standpoint. As a wealthy nation, we are duty bound to give every American a first-class education. Everyone will not make it to Harvard, which is understandable. Everyone will not become rocket scientists, and we are aware of this too. Nevertheless, there are those who will be able to learn marketable skills. This nation is in need of skilled workers and craftswomen. It is the responsibility of America to educate, train, and make use of those trained American citizens.

Educating and training people at lower levels and sending them on their way is the appropriate things to do. I stand to be corrected, but as far as I know, this isn't the case.

Skilled workers are hard to find in the United States. This is why many American companies look overseas for skilled workers. These expatriates came in and took jobs that American workers should have been doing.

If this nation produces skilled engineers and technologists, where are they? Why turn to developing nations to find skilled workers? Unfortunately, we should take the blame for this dilemma. Why isn't corporate America hiring and training Americans? This is something to think about. Is it because of greed, a lack of vision, or both? Whatever the reason or reasons, it is an indication that corporate America is only interested in profit, profit, and more profit.

Let's take inner cities and rural areas for example. Are the people who are lagging behind untrainable? I don't believe they are.

I saw a young black person cutting grass the other day, and I mentioned that he could do better than cutting grass on a full-time basis to make a living. He looked at me with tears in his eyes and said, "All I want is a chance to do something better than cutting grass." I was moved with compassion.

He is not alone. There are thousands of young people just like him. They are looking for a chance to do better, but where is the help and assistance? What can be done about this national dilemma? They can't find skilled American workers for domestic, commercial, and industrial jobs while young able-bodied men and women hopelessly roam the streets?

I have the answer to this problem. America is in need of an apprenticeship program that trains young men and women to become expert workers. Many prosperous nations have such programs. The program would empower people from inner cities and rural areas who are at the lower economic levels of society—those who are lagging behind. I invite the powers that be to take this suggestion seriously and see what happens.

This nation would prosper, and robberies would be less frequent. Those at the lower levels of the economic spectrum would rise, and there would be no need to depend on people from developing nations to come in and take American jobs. In this case, the masses would be empowered to have a sense of economic direction.

This is the hope and desire of every American. When there is no vision, the people will be sure to perish. This means that we should anticipate things long before they actually happen. Shortsightedness is a problem in this country. Many of us are confused by technology. We tend to keep up with the latest equipment, but we fail to think constructively. This is one reason we are in the dilemma we are in as a nation. Many people failed to anticipate what would happen if certain condition weren't met. Many people don't see what would happen if they failed to apply adequate lubricant to the engine of the vehicle they were operating think about what would happen if they drove while intoxicated. Short memories, lack of paying attention to detail, and lack of preparation for the future are some of the problems with the American people. I could have cited many more deficiencies. Many people aren't thinking or making wise and prudent decisions. I pray that these things will change for the good of this nation and its people.

The proposal by corporate America to replace black American workers with workers from India, the Philippines, and other Asians nations leaked. This proposal, true or false, was that many executives intended to bring in Asian workers to replace black Americans. It's clear that this plan didn't pan out very well, but there has been some minor success in the undertaking. Some workers from the above-mentioned, and other nations are here working in America, but the grand intention by corporate America to replace black workers with Asians workers didn't go well. Instead, corporate America turned their attention to people from Central and South America. Many of these people can be seen all around, especially on local and national news. The gradual phasing out of black workers for Latinos seems to be gaining momentum. It would be a good idea for government to look into the matter.

Whatever the reason or reasons behind this thinking, it should be investigated. We are aware that the masses aren't been properly educated and trained. The use and abuse of opioids is another factor. Our educational system leaves much to be desired. This makes many people who are lagging behind those from other nations more noticeable. We must get our house in order in terms of our educational system—or we will be in trouble. People from inner cities and rural areas weren't given the proper educational opportunities in the first place. To add insult to injury, they weren't given marketable skills. What do we, as a civilized society, expect of these people when we aren't educating or training them?

It should never be forgotten that injustice has negative consequences. In addition, it should never be forgotten that the eyes of the universe see all things. Rewards and punishments are the facts of life. Rewards and punishments apply to people, organizations, cities, states, and nations. There are no exceptions to this rule. The dilemmas facing this nation and its people are taking a toll. The

American people are to be blamed. We should be mindful of the fact that we will reap what we have sown. Ignorance of providential laws is no excuse.

This brings us to the dumbing down of this nation and its people.

The Dumbing Down of America

You are now aware of many troubles and trials facing this nation and its people. Before we continue, let's contemplate a statement that was made by the Mayor of New York City sometime in 2011. The Mayor criticized the behavior of blacks and Latino men. He goes on to say, "this enormous cohort of black and Latino males who don't know how to behave in the workplace and don't have any prospectus." The Mayor is perfectly correct! I addressed young black men behavioral issues in my books. Books such as: " *A Message to Black America: Motivating Young Inner- City Black Men to Excellence.*" Why they aren't reading the books is not known. Where are the black intellectuals, and why aren't they involved in young black men's issues?

I reached out to African Americans leaders such as: officials in the NAACP, AME Church, BET, and many representatives in the black society across the nation, but to no avail. At times, I felt as though I am a lonely voice crying in the wilderness, trying to motivate black men who are lagging behind! The books are there, but I cannot receive the help I need in bringing them to inner-city people. People in the news media aren't concerned about the plight of those who are left behind! If you don't have the money, you are out of luck with those people!

Statistics reveal that crime takes place almost always in minority neighborhoods. This is something that has been going on for a long time. It's time that the black American society wake up and be accountable for the behavior of their people. The black society will not come of age until those at the lower level are lifted up to be on par with their middle class counterparts!

JAMES A. HUDSON

Dumbing Down By Technology

Now you should be aware of another major dynamic: the dumbing-down process that is in progress. This has to do with technology and other things. The dumbing-down of this nation and its people is moving into higher gear. I will bring to your attention the many elements behind this dynamic. Most of these elements are generated in this country. In this regard, we will look at the dumbing-down by electronics and,other technology.

There was a time, not long ago, when one could call the telephone operator and speak to a live person. All this has changed, and these are things of the past. There are change in this area due to automation. Automation in the telephone communication business has singlehandedly destroyed middle-class American workers in this industry. Corporate America, commerce, and other industries are all fully automated in terms of technology in this industry. One would be hard pressed to call any organization and connect with a live person. Instead, one will go around in an endless loop of recordings. I am not against automation, however, when this technology is designed and deployed to replace American workers, that is a dilemma. It threatens the livelihoods of many Americans. Technology has replaced tens of thousands of American middle-class workers because of the greed and arrogance of the elites in this country.

The image above depicts women telephone switchboard operators at work in Helena. This was one of Bell telephone exchange facility out of thousands that were once located all across the country employing thousands of people. With the advent of automation, thousands of these people were out of work. Thus, the beginning of the destruction of middle-class Americans workers.

But this is not all.

Once upon a time utility companies, including electric power companies, employed thousands of men and women throughout this country to read electric meters. Unfortunately, this has changed in many states, and it is changing in many others states as well. Power companies turned to automation to read electric meters and replaced workers who were assigned to read electric meters. They installed 'fiber-optic cables' between electric meters and their central administrative offices. In this case, they are able to read meter from their facilities through automation. There are no more meter readers as we knew them in the past. The people who were making a living reading your meters have been phased out. The moral of the story is that they have lost their jobs. They lost their jobs just as those telephone operators did.

These are some of the things that are taking place in America in recent time. This is only the tip of the iceberg. Robots are coming to take the rest of the jobs from the American workers. To add insult to injury, soon there will be driver-less cars, tractor trailers, school buses, and dump trucks. In this case, those who are making a living driving these vehicle will soon be out of work. And so, the dumbing down of this nation and its people is in progress.

Have you considered the social harm that's been done to the younger generation of Americans through the advent of technology? For example, in the home parents and children don't communicate in any meaningful ways anymore due to the advent of the iPad, iPhone, computer, X box etc. The gadgets take priority over meaningful dialogue. These things happen in schools and other public places as well.

If these things are allowed to continue, the dumbing down of this nation will continue to weaken the family structure of the

American people. Before long, American civilization will be nothing but a distant memory. And so we see from the above, as well as many other factors, that the declining process is fully established! The elite, the ruling-class, and the government are to be blamed for these scourge on the people.

Another factor ruining this nation is greed and selfishness. You probably are aware of this, nevertheless, let me bring you up to date on some interesting developments that you may, or may not be aware of.

Selfishness and Greed

Greed, selfishness, and dishonesty are dragging down this nation. Everyone seems to be concerned about themselves and their connections rather than for the general good of their fellow Americans. Even those who are in charge of making laws, rules, and regulations are no exception. People making laws often do it so that the laws they passed are advantageous to them. This was brought to your attention earlier. On the other hand, in connection with people doing business, this is not to say that people in business shouldn't make a fair profit. Nevertheless, a fair profit and wanton greed and dishonesty are unfair practices.

People doing things for their own advantage—regardless of the negative consequences to others—is not entirely new. What is new is the admission of guilt by many people. Many Americans engage in the self-interest dynamic as presented above, are not doing these things in the best interest of the general welfare, and well-beings of the Americans peoples.

Let's look into this homeowners association concept to get a better understanding of greed.

People Are Out for Themselves

Homeowner associations (HMO) are a startling reminder of what people who make laws, rules, and regulations are capable of doing. I live in an area that's under the jurisdiction of a homeowner's association. Frankly, I don't know what I am paying this HMO fees for. They aren't doing squat for us, but every month, we will have to pay the association fees. Above all, it's pointless to take HMO to court. You cannot win. Judges make it plain: "if you do not like the association, you should be removed."

Well, this brings us to the problem of never-ending lawsuits in America. The United States is said to be the lawsuit capital of the civilized world. There is some truth to this belief. Americans are well known for suing the pants off their fellow Americans. No other nation is caught in this sort of unpleasant undertaking. If your dog makes what can be considered unnecessary noise, your neighbor will sue. If the volume of your stereo is considered too high, you can expect to be sued by your neighbor. These are minor examples on the domestic level. On the corporate level, being sued and suing others happen constantly. There is no end in sight.

I am of the opinion that many people are on a get-rich-quick scheme. Many people are after easy money. Unfortunately, these are some of the elements that set brother against brother in this country. Frankly, these people and other schemers are destroying this nation and its people.

Scheming is another curse upon this nation and its people. There are people in this country who have the audacity to form schemes to defraud others of their money and other possessions. Do these people believe they can inflict harm on others and go free? Aren't they aware of the all-seeing eyes of the Almighty? Many of these people lose it all in the long run and end up behind bars and disgraced. Many of these dishonest people commit suicide. This brings us to this biblical question: "What will it profit a people to gain the whole world and lose his only soul?" Nothing, zero, zilch. They will gain no profit in the end.

This brings us to the news media. The behavior of some of the news media in this country is despicable. We should call them out for what they are.

JAMES A. HUDSON

The Influence of the News Media

The news media in this country is out of control. Have you considered the rotten job that's been done by many media outlets in this country? Many people in the news media aren't afraid of expressing their bias for one and their support for another. This is evident by watching, reading, and listening to them. At times, it would appear as if they are fanning the flames of hatred against the political party they don't favor while elevating and promoting their favorite ones. People in this industry aren't concerned about public perception of their favoritism for one and their dislike for the other. Their disparaging comments about one political party and acceptance of the other promulgates vices, disputes, and strife.

There was a time when one could rely on the news for truthfulness, accuracy, and impartiality. Unfortunately, those days are over. For the most part, one cannot believe what these people are communicating to the public. Accuracy is a thing of the past. There people aren't reporting as much as giving their own opinions.

In terms of local and national dilemmas, it's clear that the news media and those within that circle aren't in the business of solving local or national problems. This is evidenced by their bad reporting and their unwillingness to offer solutions to the nation's dilemmas. There are so many dilemmas facing this nation, yet these people have no solutions to offer, no suggestion and no remedy for the cure of the ill of the nation and its people! When there is a disaster, natural or man-made, they are the first on the scene. They pounce on the scene like turkey vultures. They often point live microphones and cameras in the faces of the victims. I would like to see the news media in this country do better. I would like to see people in this business bring people together rather that dividing them. They should be offering solutions to local and national problems rather than criticizing.

I have nothing against these people in the news business, but I don't admire the way many of them are doing their business. Impartiality and vice foment resentment, and resentment is the lot for many of those in the news media in this country today.

DECLINING UNITED STATES THE RISING REPUBLIC OF CHINA

This chapter presented fundamental information in connection with the troubles facing this nation and its people. You are now aware of many minor and major dilemmas affecting this nation, preventing it from remaining on the summit of greatness. The dynamics behind the state of affairs in inner- cities and rural areas were revealed to you. The necessary steps to eradicate poverty and ignorance were also presented. Injustice perpetuated by the powers that be against people at the lower ends of the economic spectrum were also brought to light. Problems relating to opioid abuse by many Americans were revealed. Demonic strongholds are often a factor in narcotics addictions issues. The rotten job that's been done by the news media was also brought to light. Cries perpetuated by inner-city blacks, and others, were discussed.

The next chapter will continue to present the case in connection with the declining United States. I will draw a parallel between failed nations and the declining of this nation and its people. The rising of the People's Republic of China will be brought to your attention as well.

CHAPTER 4

Rise and Fall of Empires

Countries rise, and countries fall, however, the earth will abide forever. The earth will abide only if the conditions are right. We will look into this dynamic later. No nation is immune from decay. Ever since people first inhabited the earth, the cycle of increase and decrease has been in motion. The rising and falling processes are natural phenomena. This naturally applies to people and the environment. People will reach their peaks and decline, in terms of the aging. The unstoppable aging process is in motion. Nations that have declined often unwittingly brought about their own demise. These things will become clear in this chapter.

I will continue to make the case in connection with the declining process of America.

This chapter covers the decline of four mighty empires: Egypt, Greece, Rome, and Great Britain.

We will also look at China to understand what they are doing, in terms of its rising.

The rising of China will undoubtedly be one of the great dramas of the twenty-first century. China's extraordinary economic growth and active diplomacy are already transforming East Asia, and future decade will see even greater increases in Chinese power and influence. But exactly how this drama will play out is the question.

Will China overthrow the existing order or become a part of it? And what, if anything, can the United States do to maintain its position as China rises? Some observer believe that the Americans era is coming to an end, as the Western-oriented world order is replaced by increasingly dominated by the East. As China gets more powerful and the United States' position erodes.

We will also draw a parallel between the rise and fall of these four nations or empires and the decline of the United States of America. Nations have risen and remained dominant for a period of time and then gradually—or suddenly—plummeted into ruin. What's the reason for this phenomenon? The common link between them will be identified. These ancient empires were superpowers that conquered other nations. We will explore the reasons they are in ruins.

The Planet Earth

The earth is a small planet in the solar system. The condition on earth must be right to sustain life. If the earth is out of balance for any reason, life will be in jeopardy. In fact, providential revelation presented in chapter 2 revealed that the earth is indeed out of balance!

> *As long as the earth endures, seed time and harvest, cold and heat, summer and winter, and day and night will not cease. (Genesis 8:22)*

This promise will only be possible if the earth endures. What would the consequences be if the earth failed to produce food for its humans and animals? What if there was no heat or cold or day or night on the earth? Things as we know them today would vanish. Life on this planet would cease to exit.

All the elements necessary to sustain people and animals are in place on earth. This is not the case with other planets. And so the proposal of venturing to planets beyond our own raises many questions.

The dynamics of misfortune are the factors behind the reality of life. Nations are no exception. The universe is so structured that we will be sure to reap that which we have sown. This includes people, cities, towns, and nations. To better comprehend the logistics behind the decline of these nations in question, we will briefly study their history.

Research has shown that the common denominators between the falls of these ancient empires included irreverence to the Divine, cruelty, inhumane treatment, and taking the lives of others. Failure to showe reverence to Ten Commandments probably was a contributing factor too. Repentance was probably not sought in this regard. Failing to recognize the functions of the universe—and adhering to its principles—has consequences.

People have three primary responsibilities on his earth: venerate the Almighty Maker, assist and do good to other people, and replenish and cultivate the earth. These are the commands that were given to Noah and his descendants after the flood.

After Noah's flood, the earth was void of people and beasts. Every living thing was destroyed except the party of Noah. Noah's party consisted of his three sons—Shem, Ham, and Japheth—and their wives. In addition, animals and birds in the ark were saved.

Noah and his three sons were instructed to go and replenish the earth. These divine instructions are the duty for humankind. No instruction was given to set foot on Heavenly body.

A Fundamental History of Former Empires

Let's briefly study the history of four nations that were once mighty empires. These empires conquered and dominated many nations before they eventually declined.

We will begin with the Egyptian Empire. Egypt was once a mighty empire. Its ancient remnants corroborate the facts. Egypt once flourished in agriculture, architecture, astronomy, medicine, and engineering. The most important element, though, was left out of the equation. This important element was the failure of the Egyptians to venerate the Divine. The Egyptians did not believe in a Supreme Being. The pharaohs regarded themselves as gods, and they were worshiped by the Egyptian people as such.

Could it be then that the decline of the Egyptian Empire was the intervention of Providence? This seems to be the case, since providential intervention brought the Israelites out of Egypt. The Israelites were slaves in Egypt for more than four hundred years. After divine intervention, they were freed and.

Many of us are familiar with the Israelites' bondage in Egypt and their freedom from the pharaoh and his Army. In addition, the Holy Scriptures give graphic accounts of the historical events in the book of Exodus.

The nations and people who fail to venerate the Supreme Being will not prosper. They might prosper for a season, but they will eventually fail. Are the American people turning away from the Divine? If this is the case, we should reconsider the consequences. Are we turning away from the power that granted us prosperity and power? I am referring to the powers that brought the flood in the days of Noah. Biblical history revealed that the flood destroyed every living thing except Noah, his family, and selected animals and birds. It was further revealed that the people in those days were ungodly, among other things. The Lord wiped them from the earth. As far as I am concerned, that was the first judgment on earth—and it will not be the last.

This nation is collapsing under the pressure of hatred. No prayer is permitted in public places. The removal of religious observations from public schools and other public institutions has had negative effects on students and on society due to a lack of tolerance and discipline.

Our schools may be one of the last places that will instill religious values in younger generations because instability in the home and family is on the rise. Instability in the home environment does not guarantee that children will be taught religious values and godly principles in the home.

Religion is an integral part of life. It points us in the right and proper direction. Religion instills love for others, patience, tolerance, and veneration for the Almighty Maker. Values related to parameters were brought to your attention. They are based on the Ten Commandments. Many younger people lack many of the qualities that religion and religious values instilled.

Ancient Egypt

The giant pyramids, massive temples, and impressive tombs of ancient Egypt tell an exciting story. A great nation rose to power and prestige more than five thousand years ago, but it crumbled after 2,500 years of triumph and glory. Today, the remnants of Egypt's great engineering marvels still astound the world. Many Westerners traveled to Egypt to study the pyramids and other ancient monuments and went insane. They ended up in mental institutions after trying to decipher the ancient Egyptians' secrets.

What is the reason behind this phenomenon? Why do Westerners go crazy in pursuit of Egypt's ancient secrets and mysteries? Could it be that the secrets in Egypt should remain there and not to be exported to the rest of the world? In any event, it's clear that the ancient Egyptians were mighty and are full of secrecy and mysteries.

For the sake of history, you should understand that the ancient Egyptians were almost always black. Today's Egyptians are a mixture of black and Arab and black and European due to colonization and interracial marriages.

Egypt is located in the northwest corner of Africa. The Sinai Peninsula extends into Asia. In AD 642, Muslim troops from Arabia captured Alexandria, the capital of Egypt. At the time of the conquest, Egypt was a province of the Byzantine or East Roman Empire. For the next two hundred years, Egypt was a province of the Arab Empire.

By the mid-800s, the Arab-Muslim rulers in Baghdad (today the capitol of Iraq) began to lose control over the territory. For most of the period between 868 and 969, Turkish dynasties governed Egypt. In 969, the Fatimids from the Tunisian coast of North Africa conquered Egypt. The Fatimids were a rival of the Abbasid Dynasty in Baghdad. They claimed to be descended from Mohammad, the founder of Islam, through his daughter, Fatima.

Egypt was developed as a nation in about 3100 BC. Egypt was divided into smaller states that finally combined into two larger ones, which we know as Upper and Lower Egypt.

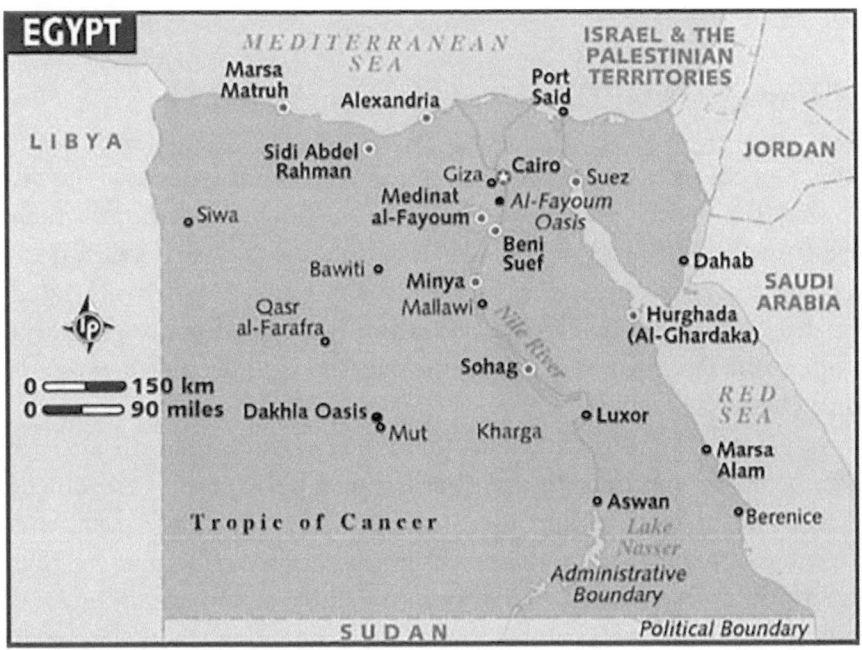

Egypt, officially the Arab Republic of Egypt, spans the southwest corner of Asia by a land bridge formed by the Sinai Peninsula. Egypt is a Mediterranean country bordered by the Gaza Strip and Israel to the north. The population of Egypt was 38,688,164 in 2012.

The trend of rising and falling empires is a reality, and that trend continues today. Weaker nations have always been invaded and taken over by more powerful ones. Egypt was trampled by many other nations many times.

What were the Egyptians doing wrong to contribute to their decline? They may have brought their decline upon themselves by their actions or inaction—or both. One shouldn't believe that the

United States is immune from decay. The prudent thing would be to seek to have Providence on our side instead of alienating the higher powers that govern the universe.

The Greek Empire was also a mighty one in the ancient world. This former mighty empire brought its civilization to the Western Hemisphere. The influence of Greek culture on the West is profound. The history of Greece is next in line.

A Fundamental History of the Greek Empire

Greece is a mountainous country in southwestern Europe. It was the center of a powerful and far-flung civilization, which explains the influence of the Greek culture on Western civilization. Greece still commands respect from many nations and is shrouded in deep mystery. The Greek civilization boasted of many gods and goddesses. There are numerous monuments to their unknown gods and goddesses.

Notwithstanding the many gods and goddesses that the ancient Greeks could summon to their beck and call, the empire crumbled. Their ruined temples and monuments to their gods are testament to the many gods and goddesses they worshipped. It's apparent that worshipping the Supreme Creator of the universe was not an integral part of ancient Greek philosophy. Thus, the fall of their empire is there for all to see.

Recorded history of Greece dates back to about 3000 BC. Greece was the heart of the Byzantine Empire. The Ottoman Turks broke this up in 1453 with their army. In that year, the Turks conquered Constantinople and created an empire of their own. Due to this conquest, many natives fled and settled throughout the Mediterranean region, in England, and in southern Russia.

The ancient Greeks were the first people to develop a democratic way of life. More than two thousand years ago, they promoted the idea that every citizen should take an active part in government. The Greeks were advanced more than any that had come before—except for the Egyptians. Today, the remnants of Greece's mighty structures still stand, testifying to their greatness, achievements, and philosophies.

The questions that remain unanswered are the causes behind the collapse of this ancient nation.

If my people who are called by my name should turn from their wicked ways and pray to me and seek my face, I will hear from heaven and heal their land.

This was not the case for the nations mentioned above. They were worshiping strange gods and goddesses, which brought the wrath of God on them.

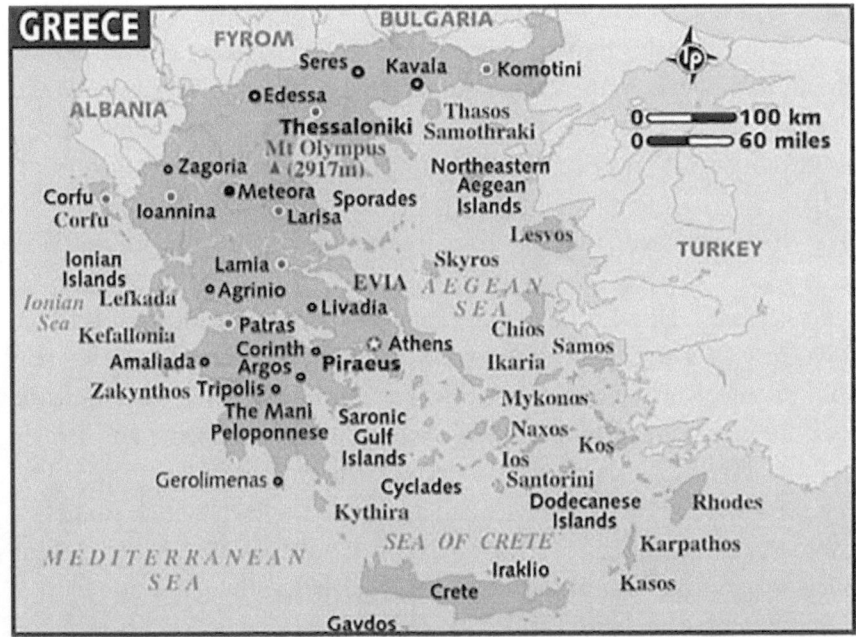

Greece, officially the Hellenic Republic, also known as Hellas, is located in southern and southeast Europe. Greece has a population of approximately eleven million as of 2016. Athens is the nation's capital and the largest city in Greece.

This brings us to the Roman Empire, which might have been more powerful than Egypt and Greece. Let's study the history of Rome and learn from its mistakes.

A Brief History of Rome

Ancient Rome was truly impressive. Even modern Rome seems to cast a spell over the rest of the world in no uncertain ways. Christians and non-Christians alike are aware of the part Rome played in ancient history. Many people don't deny that the Crucifixion took place. Is Jesus the Messiah that he proclaimed himself to be? The answer to the question varies depending on one's religious perceptions and philosophies.

I'm not seeking to convert readers to Christianity or compelling them to believe in biblical and spiritual things. Everyone should decide according to his or her faith and beliefs. Nevertheless, I will shed light on history as it is documented in the archives of biblical facts.

Rome played a major role in the history of the Crucifixion as it relates to Jesus, the Christ. The Roman soldiers were the ones who actually nailed him to the cross. Emperor Constantine was the governor of a province in Rome during the birth of Jesus. Roman soldiers received their instructions from him. Julius Caesar Augustus was the governor of that territory, which is now Palestine and Israel.

As far as Christians are concerned, the Romans were responsible for the Crucifixion of the Messiah and not the Jews, which is alleged by many people. However, the Jewish people rejected Jesus as their Messiah and handed him over to be crucified.

During the birth of Jesus, the Romans were occupying the landmass known today as Israel, Palestine, Egypt, and Mesopotamia (now Iraq), and many other nations in the Middle East. Rome has a long and bloodied history of terror and oppression. To top it off, the ancient Roman rulers were ruthless and cruel. Times have changed, and so did the Roman rulers. Not long ago, Pope John Paul II went on a pilgrimage to the Middle East to apologize to the Muslims for the atrocities carried out by the Romans. He apologized openly and fervently to the Muslim community for atrocities committed by the ancient Romans against the Muslim people.

The Romans once occupied the Muslim territories, enslaved the people, tortured them, converted them to Christianity, and killed those who refused to be converted. The Romans brutalized and oppressed them mercilessly. To the dismay of Christians around the world, the Muslims refused to accept Pope John's Paul II forgiveness. Their hatred for Rome and the Roman Catholic Church continues.

The Muslims seem to be unforgiving people. They are unforgiving to those who have done them wrong, but this is not the proper attitude. Their religion seems to forbid forgiveness. They believe they are doing the will of God by killing others as well as themselves. Often, they will blow up themselves and others with deadly explosive devices, believing their spirits will go to heaven to reap their just rewards. To Christians, this belief system is ridiculous. Nothing could be further from the truth they proclaim.

Jesus taught Christians that they should love their enemies and do good to those who hate them and spitefully use them. This command is a far contrast to the Muslim belief. Their hatred for Christians in general and Roman Catholics in particular continues.

In terms of history, the Roman Empire was probably the largest empire of its kind in the ancient world. The Roman Empire included most of Europe, the Middle East, the northern coastal area of Africa, and part of Asia. As the Roman Empire conquered nations, millions of people who spoke different languages and worshiped different gods became part of the Roman Empire. The military powers and government of Rome united the people and kept them in check by stern force, torture, and even death.

Although the Roman Empire fell apart almost 1,600 years ago, it still influences our lives today. The Roman Catholic Church influences the world in a profound way. Rome is the home of the Vatican, the main Roman Catholic Church. Today, there are more than 400 million Roman Catholic around the globe.

More than three hundred million people speak languages that are directly related to Latin, the Roman tongue. Many words in the

English language and other languages come from Latin. Roman law provided the basis of the laws of most European and Latin American nations. One can understand the power of the former empire today.

The ancient Romans' desire for conquest brought great misery to many weaker nations. Its military forces brought hardship and death to millions of people around the world. The rulers of Rome were brutal dictators who ruled with iron hands. It should be remembered that the boundaries of the ancient Roman Empire changed many times during its 1,300-year reign as a mighty empire.

Rome once ruled all the lands around the Mediterranean Sea. This includes Spain, Portugal, France, Belgium, the Netherlands, and most of England and Wales. Switzerland, Australia, and the Balkans were Roman territories as well. Countries such as Yugoslavia, Romania, Bulgaria, Albania, and Greece once were Roman territories.

One can only imagine the power and influence of this once great empire. Roman soldiers did not invade and take over nations without a fight. However, with as powerful and invincible as this ancient empire was, it eventually fell. Today, many countries dislike Rome. Nevertheless, this nation still exists. The former Roman Empire was once a force to reckoned with.

It appears to have taken a divine intervention to bring down this former wicked empire. Today, the influence of modern Rome seems to be centered on the principles of Christianity and religious teachings. The leader of the Roman Catholic Church is the pope. It is generally believed that the pope is the true representative of Christ on earth. The pope is referred to as "the holy father."

The Roman Empire was a remarkable achievement. It had a population of sixty million people spread across lands encircling the Mediterranean and stretching from northern England to the sunbaked banks of the Euphrates, and from the Rhine to the North African cost.

Let's turn our attention to another former ancient empire, the British Empire. As the song goes, "Roll, Britannia, Britannia rules the waves, we shall never, never, never be a slave?" Britain was a force to be reckoned with in terms of military powers on land, on the seas, and in the air.

A Brief History of the British Empire

No one thought the mighty British Empire would fall. Today, Britain is far from being a superpower. This tiny island nation once dominated most of the world with its military power. If it were not for the colonies that sustained England, she would have been decline many centuries ago. Although many of the nations Britain once colonized became Commonwealth nations, most of these nations eventually returned to self-governing, independent from Brain. Many are still trading with England and supplying goods and services to keep Britain economically viable.

Britain was a powerful nation indeed, but it has declined like Egypt, Greece, and Rome.

Britain may be down, but it is not out by any stretch of the imagination. Britain is a close ally of the United States of America, and British citizens colonized the United States. Both nations are closely related in many respects. Britain still maintains a powerful military force and is capable of inflicting grievous harm on less developed nations. England is a staunch ally of the United States and depends on the United States for military protection for the most part.

England is a relatively small island nation. For hundreds of years, it has been one of the most important countries in the world. The English people are inventive and creative; they brought about the Industrial Revolution, which raised the standard of living in many nations. English people invented the modern jet engine in the nineteenth century. The British have invented many things, and credit should be given to them accordingly.

England joined Wales, Scotland, and Northern Ireland to form the United Kingdom of Great Britain and Northern Ireland. London is the capital of England and the capital of the United Kingdom. The euro is the currency of the United Kingdom.

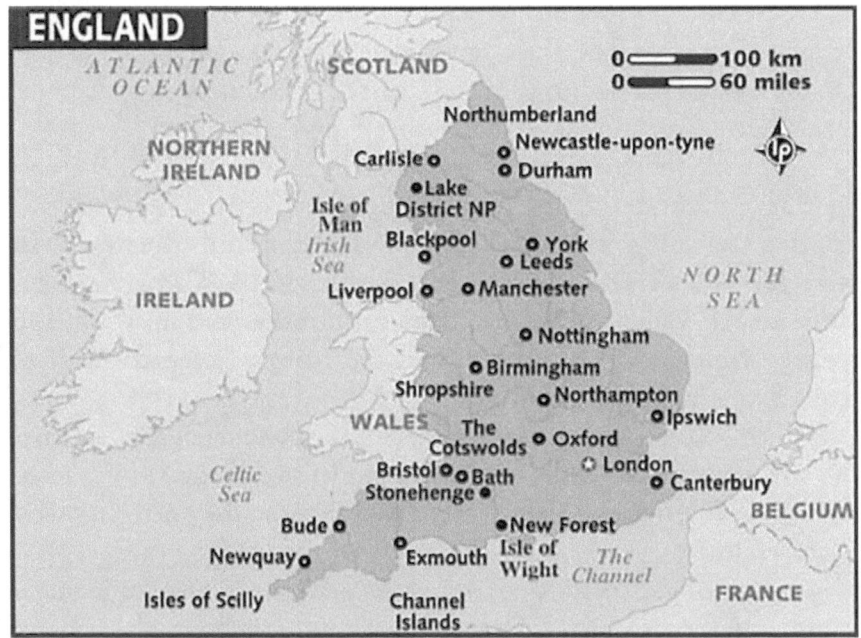

England is part of the United Kingdom. It shares a border with Wales to the west and Scotland to the north. The Irish Sea lies to the west of England, and the Celtic Sea is to the southwest. The population of England as of 2016 was 55.27 million.

The English people were great explorers too. Their fearless sailors, traders, and colonists carried their language, law, government, and customs around the globe. England became the mother country of the English-speaking nations as well as the United States of America. They gave the world the English language as we know it today. The legacy of Great Britain reaches far and wide.

British people founded the United States of America. In addition, Canada, Australia, and New Zealand were colonized by the British. English inventors made the Industrial Revolution possible. It raised the standards of living in almost every corner of the globe. England is an important ally of many nations, including the United States and Canada.

The history of Great Britain goes back hundreds of years, but no one knows with certainty when people first set foot on that island.

In any event, the Iberian people were probably the first people to occupy that land. The Iberians lived during the Old and the New Stone Age and learned to use flint stone to make tools and weapons. They grew crops and raised cattle, sheep, pigs, and dogs.

Did the Iberian create Stonehenge or inherit it? Early Iberians were at peace until the first invaders, the Celts, arrived. In 1600 BC, the first Celts from central Europe invaded England (the first Celts were the Gales.) The second invaders include the Cymry and the Britons. The Gales pushed the Iberians into the wild northern and western regions of the country, and the Britons accepted most of what is now England and Wales.

The island was again invaded and conquered by another outside power in AD 43. The Roman emperor, Claudius, conquered Britannia, defeated the Celts, and moved them to the north and west of the country.

The Romans organized Britain as a province and built many camps and fortresses to crush any other invaders who might attempt to displace them. The camps and fortresses couldn't prevent another invasion. Britain was invaded next by the Germans. As the Germans swept into England, they pushed the Britons westward. The Britons were defeated many times and were pushed into the mountainous regions of Cornwall, Wales, and Scotland.

The Germanic tribes were organized in small nations. Jutes lived in Kent; the Saxons occupied southern England, which is now divided into East Saxons, Middle Saxons, South Saxons, and Sussex.

The Romans once invaded and conquered England. The ancient Romans were truly a warlike people. It's no wonder the British people despised the Romans. The history of Britain is long and bitter, but Britain rose to conquer most of the world, including Rome. Britain has fallen in a manner similar to Egypt, Greece, and Rome.

Countries rise and fall, but the earth will abide forever—or until Providence deems it necessary to bring an end to the existence of mother earth and its inhabitants.

"The wicked shall perish." Many God-fearing people are familiar with this divine proclamation. No one—no nation—will escape this proclamation. It is a fact that everyone should be aware of. This should be at the forefront of the mind before engaging in evil, lawlessness, or deception. The proclamation has brought down nations that were unjust and harmful to other nations and their people.

I am not opening up old wounds to highlight the wicked deeds of the nations that brought harm to their nations and their people. We are tracing the common link that runs through failed and failing nations.

If there is one lesson that should be learned from these rising and falling nations, it is that none of these empires were God-fearing nations at that point. History recorded their unfair practices, and brutality, torture, and death were standard practices in those days. They had no fear of God or reverence for the Divine in their governments.

Subdue and conquer was the order of the day, and many nations are waiting in the wings to subdue and conquer other nations. There are nations seeking to acquire automatic weapons for the destruction of other nations. One nation in the Middle East is currently seeking to acquire nuclear weapons in order to "wipe other nations off the map" as its leader proclaimed to the world in a televised broadcast. This nation in question doesn't necessarily want to subdue and conquer that nation that its leader deems an enemy. It wants to destroy that nation because of religious and cultural differences.

Such ill will has not been seen since the beginning of time. People's inhumanity toward their fellow humans has not disappeared completely. This is true in the Middle East and in the Western Hemisphere.

In this chapter, we examined the early history of four ancient empires. We studied their rises and falls. "The fear of the Lord is the beginning of wisdom." No nation will prosper when its people fail to fear God.

Are the American people failing to venerate our Almighty Maker? If this is the case, how can we ever hope to continue prospering? One of the immediate actions that can be taken is the return of religious worship in public schools and other public institutions.

In the next chapter, we will look at the relevance of exploring distant planets when there is work to be done on earth. People are in need, not just here in this country, but around the world. I will continue to present the evidence in connection with the declining process of this nation.

CHAPTER 5

No Profit, No Gain: Exploring Distant Planets

People were given specific instructions by the Divine to go and replenish the earth. This command was given to Noah and his descendants after the destruction of the earth by the flood. Since then, the population of the earth been increasing steadily.

As of January 2020, the population of the earth is approximately 7.7 billion, and the population of the United States is approximately 345 million. The population of the earth is expected to increase to 1.2 billion by 2100 (just under 9 billion). This increase will burden the existing worldwide resources. Thus, promulgate additional poverty, starvation, disease, and ignorance. It will add to the current dilemma facing the world, especially in underdeveloped and developing nations. This is not limited to the United States and its current and future populations.

Overpopulation of the earth, plundering of the sea, pollution of the air etc, were cited by Divine providence. "These things cannot be allowed to continue declared the angel Gabriel." Do these observations indicate that the population of the earth is going to be reduce by the powers controlling the earth? Please revisit chapter 2. I pray that the Lord will not bring affliction on the earth so as to reduce the population of the earth.

It is the duty and responsibility of people on the earth to eradicate starvation and poverty. Until these requirements are met, there is work to be done on this earth that humans call home.

What is the duty and responsibility of developed and affluent nations toward poverty and starvation in underdeveloped nations? These questions should be answered. Until developed nations are able to answer these questions realistically, there is still work to be done. People should seek to develop the earth instead of venturing off to other planets and satellites.

Developed nations are duty bound to go to the aid and assistance of impoverished and underdeveloped countries. Nations are struggling to feed and shelter their people. There are many ways in which aid and assistance can be rendered to impoverished nations. We will look into these things in this chapter.

There will be no profit or gain from venturing to distant planets. People will not be able to live or do business on other planets. Can fish live on dry land? Can people live underwater? People will not be able to live on Jupiter, Mars, Venus, the moon, or any planet in the heavenly realms. What's the intention in the first place? Is it to seek and acquire treasures, gold, diamonds, and other precious elements from these planets or the moon?

Earth is the planet that was given to humans. People will probably be able to set foot on distant planets, but they will not be able to reside in outer space. The human body was designed and conditioned to live on earth. I don't regard myself as rocket scientist. I am a visionary and a good one too. I am predicting that people's willingness to live on distant planets will be in vain.

Why Not Make the Desert Bloom?

In the United States, poverty, hunger, and homelessness are constant companions to many. This is supposed to be the wealthiest nation on the earth. We have the technologies to make the desert bloom. With careful planning and development, deserts can be irrigated to produce enough food to feed all people. Enough food can be grown to feed all the children in this country. In addition, we could feed the people in developing and underdeveloped nations who lack the knowledge to do so. There is enough water that can be brought to the surface for irrigating the deserts in poor nations and in this country.

As far as people are concerned, there are three basic needs: food, clothing, and shelter. These have been the basic human needs since the beginning of time. Once these requirements are met, other things can follow suit. Lacking the basic necessities of life will pose problems. When the basic necessities are met, then the light of education can come. People will not advance until the necessities of life are met.

People have a duty and responsibility to other people. They should help others overcome obstacles and rise to their full potential. This isn't the case for the most part. Instead, we are investing a great deal of money in developing vehicles to take us to distant planets and weapons of war to eliminate others. Hardships are all around us. There are hardships to be found in inner cities and towns across this nation. In addition, many people in rural areas are struggling to survive. Again, funding for explorations of outer space could be better spent lifting people out of poverty. People in rural areas could be encouraged to produce food for national and international consumption.

People are doing a poor job of taking care of hunger and homelessness. How will people cope with population increases? Where will they find food, clothes, and shelter?

In this country, more money is wasted on nonessential things than on eliminating human suffering. Consider the donations made to politicians from both political parties. Millions of dollars are donated toward both political parties, and human needs go unmet here and in impoverished nations around the globe.

Monetary Contributions to Politics

The American people had made financial contributions to political parties that are far above expectations. These donations could be better spent in educating those at the lower ends of the economic spectrum. What about benevolence, sympathy, and love for the less fortunate?

In the past twenty or twenty-five years, billions of dollars were contributed to politicians. The money could have been spent on eradicating poverty many times over. Educational opportunities could have been given to eradicate poverty, ignorance, and homelessness, especially for American veterans.

Our veterans have served their country well. After leaving the service, many of these people ended up on the scrap heap of society. Many are disabled, jobless, and homeless. Are we a God-fearing people the way we proclaim to be? Do the rich among us care about other humans? Are the principles of Christianity and Judaism being swept under the carpet in the United States of America?

Inhumanity to other people is probably bringing grief to the Supreme Being and to the universe. This is probably a factor in the decline facing this nation and its people.

The Lord regretted that he made people. He promised that he wouldn't destroy the earth again with a flood. Will the earth soon be destroyed by fire? Will people destroy the earth with our own weapons of war? That's something to think about.

In any event, the inhumanity of people has reached the eyes of Providence. What happens next? Only time will tell. We should read the signs of the times and contemplate what lies ahead. We shouldn't marvel over the calamities that are taking place all over or the hidden secrets that are being brought to light. Things will only worsen as things that were swept under the carpet are exposed. The hearts of humans will continue to fail as nefarious forces rain terror on the sons of men:

> *See the mighty host advancing, Satan leading on: mighty men around us are falling courage almost gone.*

Those who are blessed with wealth should have compassion for those who are impoverished, homeless, or hopeless. What's it like for a rich person to pass a homeless person on the street on their way to their million-dollar mansion? What it's like for someone to know that children are going without food? People from inner cities do not have marketable skills to provide a decent living for their loved ones and themselves. Yet, these people will contribute millions to their favorite political parties and national monuments.

There are superabundant amounts of guilt to go around—from the super wealthy to the government's unnecessary spending. The government is funding nonessential projects, such as space exploration, when it should be committed to funding programs to eradicate failing schools and poverty. In terms of foreign aid, it seems to take priority over poverty and homelessness.

Education is a great light. Those who are poorly educated or not educated at all are in the darkness. Our society owes every citizen an education and marketable skills. Technical colleges and community colleges across the nation are overdue. These are some of the things that we should be investing in rather than correctional institutions. It should never be forgotten that ignorance and poverty are the roots of crime and violence.

You should have a fundamental knowledge of the important planets, stars, and moons. You have a duty to understand some of the planets and stars in our solar system. Many of them have been discovered, and many more will be discovered in the future. Those that are of interest to us will be brought to your attention.

Whatever secrets and mysteries there are to be known were revealed by the will of Providence. These things were brought to your attention earlier. Other secrets and mysteries that are intended to be known will be revealed in the course of time. The secrets and mysteries that should remain secret will never be revealed. With that in mind, let's examine the seven major heavenly bodies that you should be aware of in the celestial domain.

Planets, Stars, and the Moon

According to Revelation, we will bring to attention the day and hour in which these heavenly bodies rule, and the angels and archangels that govern each day of the week beginning with the highest (farthest from earth) and continue through to the lowest (closet to the earth). First, you should understand that the moon is a lunar object. It has no light of its own. It reflects the rays of the sun that strike its surface. The moon is a lunar satellite close to the earth, and it supposedly provokes insanity during full moon.

Please see below for images of these heavenly bodies and the days and hours in which they rule.

Saturn: from sunrise on Saturday to sunrise on Sunday. The angel over Saturday is Cassiel.

Saturn is the sixth planet from the sun and the second largest in the solar system, after Jupiter. It is a gas giant with an average radius about nine times that of Earth. Saturn is named after the Roman god of agriculture. Saturn is one of the five planets that can be seen with the naked eye. It is also the fifth brightest object in the solar system.

Jupiter: From Sunrise on Thursday to Sunrise on Friday The Angel over Thursday is Sachiel.

Jupiter is the fifth planet from the sun and is the largest in the solar system. It is a giant planet with a mass one-thousandth that of the sun, but two and a half times that of all the other planets in the solar system. Jupiter is the second brightest planet in the night sky, after Venus.

Mars: From Sunrise to Tuesday to Sunrise on Wednesday: The Angel over Tuesday is Samael.

Mars is the fourth planet from the sun and the second smallest planet in the solar system, after Mercury. In English, Mars carries the name of the Roman god of war and is often referred to as the Red Planet because the iron oxide on its surface gives it a reddish appearance that is distinctive among the astronomical bodies visible with the naked eye.

Sun: from sunrise on Sunday to sunrise on Monday. The angel over Sunday is Michael.

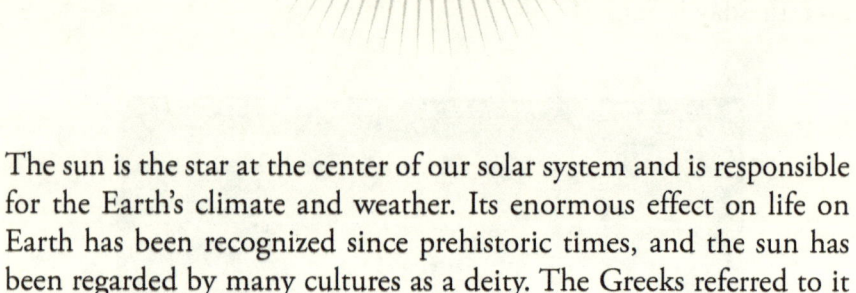

The sun is the star at the center of our solar system and is responsible for the Earth's climate and weather. Its enormous effect on life on Earth has been recognized since prehistoric times, and the sun has been regarded by many cultures as a deity. The Greeks referred to it has Helios, and the Romans called it Sol.

Venus: From Sunrise on Friday to Sunrise on Saturday: The Angel over Friday is Anael.

Venus is the second planet from the sun, orbiting it every 224.7 Earth days. It is named after the Roman goddess of love and beauty. It is the second-brightest natural object in the night sky after the sun.

Mercury: From Sunrise on Wednesday to Sunrise on Thursday: The Angel over Wednesday is Raphael.

Mercury is the smallest and innermost planet in the solar system. It is named after the Roman deity Mercury, the messenger of the gods.

Moon: From Sunrise on Monday to Sunrise on Tuesday. The Angel over Monday is Gabriel. This is the relative order in which these Heavenly bodies function. They will continue on this course until the end of time.

The moon is an astronomical body that orbits the earth, and it is the earth's only permanent natural satellite.

There are eight planets, one star, and the moon. The moon is the closest object to the earth, and people have staked claims on its surface. It's clear that people found no sustaining grace on the moon. They are done colonizing the moon and are venturing off to distant planets. It is doubtful that people will survive a voyage to these planets. If they did, they would be eager to return to earth as soon as possible.

People will not be able to live on distant planets. They might not even be able to survive the journey to Mercury. It would waste precious resources that could have been invested in eliminating poverty on earth.

The planets have dominion over the day that appeared near their names. The days of the week take their names from the day in which the planet, star, or moon rules. Each of the planets governs a specific day.

In addition, the planets, stars, and moons radiate beneficial waves that we were exposed to on the day we were born. The radiation from planets, stars, and moons are invisible, but they are effective. They can be harnessed and put to use, but the science behind this is beyond the scope of this book.

Everyone on earth was born under a planet, star, or moon. As a result, we are all influenced differently by the power of these heavenly bodies. Which planet were you born under? What is your characteristic? These are some of the dynamics related to behaviors and personalities of people. Everyone is totally different.

According to Greek and Roman mythology, Venus was the goddess of love. Since Venus rules on Fridays, Fridays are associated with love and romance. Everyone looks forward for the arrival of Friday—and I do too!

Mars is said to be the god of war, according to mythology. Tuesday is ruled by Mars. Tuesday is associated with hard labor, pain, and suffering for many. The planets, stars, and moons are associated with many legendary myths, which appear to be authentic. Other planets have their legendary myths as well, but these will have to suffice for now.

This chapter presented information that is relevant to you. People should focus on relieving poverty on earth instead of turning to distant planets. Five major planets, one major sun, and the moon—and the days they have their dominion—were revealed, together with the angel that govern each day of the week.

I also brought attention to four dominant and powerful empires. These nations declined for reasons that were presented. It is beneficial to revisit the history of the United States. People who studied American history will find it refreshing, and those who didn't will find this history lesson interesting.

In the next chapter, we will study the history of the United States of America. The republic of the United States is unique.

CHAPTER 6

Early American History

The United States is the fourth largest country on earth—both in size and in population. It is located in North America and covers an area from the Atlantic Ocean to the Pacific Ocean. The United States possessions include Alaska, which is located north of Canada, and Hawaii, which is located in the Pacific. One of the world's great wonders, the Grand Canyon, is located in the United States. The Mississippi River and Niagara Falls are in the United States of America.

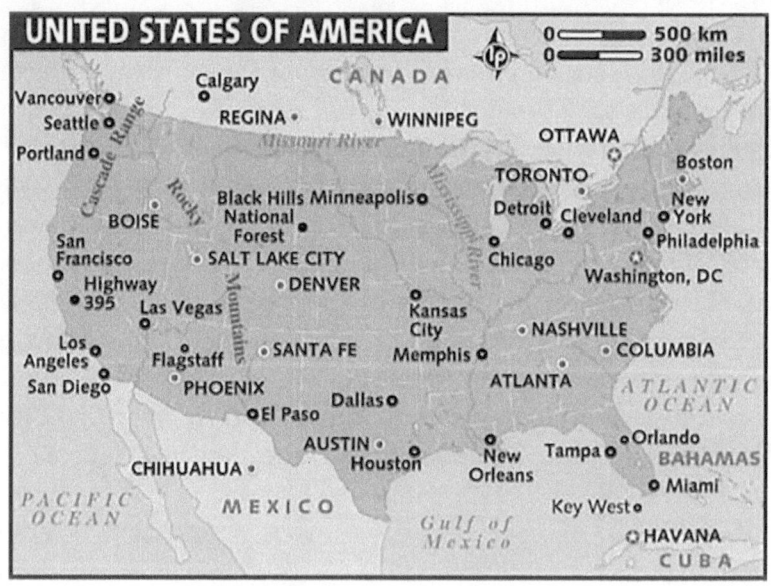

The United States of America, commonly known as the United States, is a federal republic composed of fifty states, a federal district, five major self-governing territories, and various possessions. At 3.8 million square miles and a population of more than 325 million, the United States is the world's third or fourth largest country by total area and the third most populated. The capital of the United States is Washington DC, and the largest city is New York City.

Before we continue, let's examine the difference between 'democracy and republic'. Many people are confused between the two terms.

The United States Is a Republic

The difference between a republic and a democracy is not the manner in which power is projected, but the limit to power. Both use the representational system, meaning that the citizenry is represented in the government by elected leaders. In both cases, the majority rule, however, in a republic the constitution limits the way in which government exercises power. These rights, rights of citizens, are inalienable and cannot be changed or alter by an elected government.

A republic therefore, is a form of government in which power resides with the people, and the governments ruled by elected leaders who govern according to laws designed to help citizens.

Located In North America

The United States covers 9,161,966 square kilometers of land, making it the third largest nation.

The United States is rich in natural resources: oil, natural gas, minerals, timber, and coal. The land was idle for thousands of years and was undeveloped, notwithstanding the fact that Native Americans were the occupants. About 350 to 300 years before the Europeans arrived, Native Americans roamed freely across the plains. They fished and hunted wild game, which included buffalo, deer, elk, and other animals. They were many tribes, and they set up villages and communities. These communities are now modern cities and towns across the nation.

With the arrival of Europeans, the Native American population was significantly reduced. However, many tribes can be found scattered throughout reservations across the nation today. They are marginalized, and they are on their way to extinction. Unfortunately, the government did not do much to protect or preserve these people. As a result, their cries for help went unnoticed and unanswered. This injustice is another nail in the coffin as far as dilemmas of this nation are concerned.

Inhumane treatment of the Indians must have reached up to Providence. The scars are there as testament.

The Arrival of the Europeans

The United States was created from a dense wilderness in a relatively short time. Five hundred years ago, no European settlers lived in North America. Up until about three hundred years ago, the United States did not exist as we know it today. However, during its 250-year history, the United States has developed into one of the richest and most powerful nations on earth.

The United States was created on the principle that all men have the right to life, liberty, and the pursuit of happiness. These noble concepts are the heart of our democracy.

During the 250-year history of this nation, it has attracted immigrants who came to seek a better way of life. Immigrants from across the globe immigrated to the United States of America. During the early period, the nation's founding fathers wrote a constitution for the United States. The Constitution governs many of the affairs of the government. The Constitution of the United States is unique. It dictates the rights and privileges for its citizens and noncitizens who are residing within its borders. In this day and age, it appears as though the Constitution is in need of revision. Although constitutional amendments are carried out from time to time, it's apparent that the time the document was written and the time we are living in today aren't compatible. Constitutional changes are necessary.

For a long time, Europeans were not aware of the vastness of the land they would later develop into the United States of America. American history begins when the Europeans brought their civilization to these shores in the 1500s and 1600s.

In the 1400s, many Europeans begin to sail westward in the hopes of reaching China. They wanted to sail around the world and trade with the Orient. They thought the world was round and smaller than it is. When Christopher Columbus sailed westward in 1492, he found land he believed was in the East Indies. He never believed that he had discovered a new continent. The Spanish and Portuguese seamen who came after him realized they had reached an unexplored and undeveloped land. They called the land the New World. The New World is associated with the United States of America.

The Thirteen Colonies

There were originally thirteen colonies, and the British claimed them all. Private enterprises were responsible for the newly claimed British colonies. The king of England granted charters to corporations to found and govern the chartered colonies. Most of the colonies became royal possessions. A governor was appointed by the king of England to rule and govern the colonies.

In 1585, Sir Walter Raleigh tried to establish a colony on Roanoke Island. It was not until around 1606 that colonists made the first settlement in Jamestown, Virginia. A London company sponsored a group of about 150 men to go to Jamestown. They suffered many setbacks and misfortunes, which included disease, illness, malaria, and Indian attacks. During this time, John Rolf began experimenting with tobacco. It proved viable and become popular in Europe, and the colonies became prosperous in tobacco trading. There was a need for farming the crop on a large-scale basis.

In 1619, Virginia had its own legislature. It was the first of its kind in North America. The population grew, and within twenty-five years, the population of Virginia had grown to approximately forty thousand people.

Men and women came from England as indentured servants, and they worked for other colonists to repay the cost of their passage to North America. Many of the indentured workers received their own parcels of land. They grew tobacco, and there was soon a need for a great number of workers.

In 1619, Negroes from Africa arrived in the New World on Dutch vessels. They were probably slaves who were brought from Africa. In 1660, planters began buying Negroes as slaves in large numbers. As a result of the large numbers of slaves, they eventually replaced many white people as indentured workers and plantation workers.

In March of 1770, British troops fired on a mob in Boston, killing many. It became known as the Boston Massacre. It would not be long before full-blown war erupted from the tensions between the colonists and the British.

When the British East Indian Company needed financial assistance, it was allowed to ship surplus tea to America at a low cost and sell it through its own dealers. The colonists bitterly opposed this action. First, it gave one company a monopoly and control over tea trading. In addition, it renewed the British claim that they had the right to tax colonists without their consent. Angry Bostonians threw a shipment of tea into Boston Harbor. This is known as the Boston Tea Party.

As a result of this action, the British government passed a series of acts aimed at severely punishing Bostonians. The colonists took steps to unite in self-defense against the British. They protested against what they regarded as "intolerable actions by the British government." Chaos and confusion soon erupted.

Virginia and all the other colonies—besides Georgia—sent representatives to a meeting in Philadelphia in September 1774. It was the first congressional meeting of its kind. After the meeting, a friendly petition was sent to King George III in England. The king and Parliament refused to make any concessions. That would trigger the war between America and Great Britain.

Fighting broke out between the colonists and the British at Lexington and Concord, near Boston, on April 19, 1775. Colonial troops fortified Breed's Hill in the hope of taking Boston, but the British routed them at Bunker Hill. A full-scale conflict began in earnest between Great Britain and the United States.

Declaring Independence

George Washington's army attacked the British troops in Boston for twelve months. However, many colonists hesitated to declare their independence from England. They felt some loyalty to the British Crown and hoped to settle the conflict peacefully. At the same time, the Second Continental Congress was meeting in Philadelphia. There were two new members in attendance: Benjamin Franklin and Thomas Jefferson. The two would later become presidents of United States of America.

The New England colonists, under the leadership of John Hancock, John Adams, and others, sided with Virginia and launched a movement for independence. On July 2, 1776, every colony in the Continental Congress, except New York, voted for independence. On July 4, 1776, Congress adopted the Declaration of Independence.

Among the accusations were the denial of the rights to self-govern. Emphasis was placed on the right to change or overthrow any government that denied their right to freedom, liberty, and justice. Early American colonists had declared their independence from England, but this was not the end of the story. They had to fight for their independence, face war with the British, and win if the New World should be an independent nation from Great Britain.

James Madison was elected president in 1808. During his presidency, the Union went to war with Britain. That war proved futile for both Britain and the new Union. The Union was defeated on land; it was humiliated when the British captured Washington, DC. The British lasted many battles at sea; nevertheless, they had a firm command of the ocean, and they blockaded the America coastlines.

The history of the United States is relatively calm and bloodless, except for a couple of skirmishes with the British Empire. This can be regarded as brother fighting against brothers in the truest sense of the word. This is based on the fact that the colonists were British citizens. No brother wants to destroy another brother under normal circumstances.

The question of the United States Civil War, on the other hand, cannot be considered to be a war in the truest sense of the word. It was not an outside invasion; it was a difference of opinion and practice that caused citizens in the Southern states to rebel against the federal government. The rebellion was due in part to the opposition of Southern plantation owners' unwillingness to dissolve the institution of slavery.

The Conflict between the United States and Britain

In 1812, the United States drifted into war with Great Britain under the leadership of President James Madison. This conflict was unsuccessful for both the United States and Britain. The United States was defeated on land and humiliated when Britain captured Washington, DC. The British lost many battles at sea, but they regained command of the ocean and blockaded America's coasts. The Americans captured Toronto from Britain, but they could not keep it. The British captured Detroit, but they lost it. Neither side gained very much, and the war ended in a kind of stalemate. The British left Boston in 1776. This war was centered mainly in the middle colonies.

General Williams Howe, the British commander, captured New York City that year, and Philadelphia was taken the following year. After defeating Washington on Long Island, he almost captured the American army. It seemed as if the British forces controlled an imaginary line located all the way from the Hudson River to Canada, cutting the colonies in half, but that did not materialize. Howe's troops failed to join forces with another army descending from northern Canada. Alas, General Burgoyne surrendered to

General Horatio Gates at Saratoga in October 1777. His surrender to Washington ended that part of this war in 1781.

The New America

Censuses taken in 1790 revealed that the population was just over four million people. There were more than four million European Americans living in the thirteen colonies. Slaves that were brought over were not in the count. Approximately one hundred thousand settlers ventured westward. The lack of roads and communication kept communities isolated. Stage coaches and horses were the main form of transportation. One colonist recorded that it probably took four to six weeks for the news of the Declaration of Independence to travel from Philadelphia to Charleston, South Carolina. The nation was growing rapidly, and Vermont became a state in 1791. Kentucky followed suit in 1792. Settlers continued to move westward, and by 1800, the population of Tennessee had grown to about one hundred thousand. Ohio had grown to more than fifty thousand. Prosperity grew rapidly since land was inexpensive and farming was a huge business. They experimented with many crops. Eli Whitney invented the cotton gin in 1793, and growing cotton became a lucrative business.

Sugarcane was cultivated, and sugar became an indispensable commodity. When De Bore proved that sugar could be refined successfully, sugar plantations spread throughout the state of Louisiana.

The United States grew in population, prosperity, and power, and its history continues. This is a brief history of the United States. This chapter was not intended to present a complete and chronological history of this nation. The Civil War was an historic event that should be presented to you. I will present to you the history of the Civil War before bringing this chapter to its conclusion.

JAMES A. HUDSON

The Civil War

The Civil War began when Southern troops bombarded Fort Sumter in Charleston Harbor. Many Southern states seceded from the union to form their own confederate government. It divided the country into two camps—the Confederate camp and the Union camp. People of the Southern states had threatened to leave the Union if Abraham Lincoln won the presidential election with Northern support alone. The people's fear ultimately triggered chaos and confusion.

Lincoln did win the election, and he declared that he would not abolish slavery in the Southern states. The people in the South were angry with those in the North for electing Lincoln as president. I stand to be corrected on this matter, but there seems to be some kind of animosity between people in the Northern states and those in the South. The indignance seems to continue even to this day.

Freeing the Slaves

In terms of slavery, Southern white plantation owners feared that President Lincoln would draft white people into slavery with the Negroes. This was a major factor behind seceding to form the Confederacy. As mentioned, the first state to secede from the Union was South Carolina. This was in December 1860. States that followed suit were Mississippi, Florida, Alabama, Georgia, and Louisiana. The war between Confederate troops and the Union troops took thousands of lives and caused several million dollars of damage. Southern states were almost bankrupt, so the breakaway Confederate states eventually reunited with the Union due to financial hardship. Huge areas of the South lay in ruin due to sabotage. Homes were burned, railroads were damaged, and bridges were destroyed. Southerners were destitute, and they had no choice but to return to the Union. Those were troubled times in the history of the nation.

More casualties resulted from the Civil War than the war between Britain and the United States. In any event, the Civil War brought about the freedom of the slaves. Slavery was abolished. That brought uncertainty and concerns to both Southern plantation owners and non–plantation owners alike.

Freed Slaves

The slaves were freed but found themselves in disarray, disillusion, and dismay. In the first place, they were in a dependent mode and were without rulers, money, and even habitats. Secondly, they could not read or write; they hadn't been allowed to attend school or learn a skill during their enslavement. They couldn't even assemble in church with white people. As a result of white non-acceptance of the freed slaves in religious circles, they eventually formed their own church—Southern Baptist Church, as we know it today.

Legal Segregation and Discrimination

Federal, local, and state laws allowed segregation. Therefore, the newly freed slaves were discriminated against legally throughout the nation. Unfortunately, segregation and discrimination resulted in inferiority complexes. The freed slaves were instilled with the belief that they were inferior and that they only measured up as three-quarters of a human being. Brainwashing is unfortunate, uncivilized, and unkind. Those who relegated the slaves and freed slaves to such a degrading status are unwise and should be ashamed of themselves.

The free slaves had no rights in the eyes of the law. Anyone could do evil things to them with impunity—no fear of being punished. This was an unfortunate time for black people in this nation and created moral dilemmas for white Americans.

Worse, no one would hire the ex-slaves. They were the outcasts of the society in spite of their overwhelming contributions to a prosperous nation.

For more than two hundred years, Africans were forced into slavery in America. They were engaged in farming, indenture servitude, and construction, among other things. The war was the turning point that brought about the Emancipation Proclamation. It was signed by President Abraham Lincoln as the result of this war. No compensation for the slaves/ex-slaves was mentioned in the proclamation. To this day, no reparation has been given to the descendants of the salves for the contributions that their ancestors made to the prosperity and welfare of the United States of America.

This injustice has yet to be resolved by the American government and people of European descent. This is one of many blemishes, guilt, and black eyes on society today. It is not too late for justice to be rendered. It is better to be late than never.

I strongly believe that the question of slavery and the aftermath is a stigma on our nation. In addition to the crime of segregation and discrimination against the freed slaves and their generations that followed, many terrorist groups sprang up throughout the nation, with the intention of opposing and destroying the Negroes. The KKK, skinheads, and other groups were actively taunting, tormenting, and lynching ex-slaves and their descendants. Black women were sexually abused, and black men were lynched, but no one paid the consequences for their crimes. Today, the breach of human dignity is haunting the conscience of the nation and its people.

It is written, "the sins of the fathers will visit the children to the third and fourth generations." Could this be one of the reasons that divine retribution is on this nation, if it is in the first place?

No one can deny the fact that the descendants of the slaves deserve more. These people should be enjoying an elevated lifestyle and a middle-class status. Although some corrective actions have been taken to help black Americans, it is not enough. I am referring to entitlements granted by the federal government.

I firmly believe that the descendants of the slaves should be educated, trained, and promoted at the expense of society. They should not be pushed aside while we embrace people that migrated from abroad. Foreigners should not be allowed to make good of the opportunities available over and above the black American people. However, due to oppression, many urban black people are bypassed completely. Many of them are unskilled. To fill this void, foreigners are taking advantage.

We acknowledged the fact that America needs the best and brightest in our scientific and technological communities. As a result, we are embracing immigrants that have come to this country with the knowledge we need. This may or may not contribute to the wealth and prosperity of America. Knowledge is a process of understanding and awareness that is gained through training and development. We have the technology, the ability, and the resources to train our people, including our black American citizens. We are able to train our people to be knowledgeable in science and technology, and this is what we should be doing for the black American people. This nation has an obligation to these people. If America is going to continue to be a great nation, ignorance and poverty should be eliminated from our society, lifting up the fallen, those that this nation owes an obligation to. Those are the appropriate actions to be taken. To add insult to injury, black people were drafted in this nation's civil war.

Civil War and Black Americans

The US Civil War that engulfed the nation almost 145 years ago was truly a turning point in this nation's history. As you probably are aware, this war was the result of resistance elements that opposed the freedom of the slaves.

As a result of this war, the currency in the North was inflated. This brought about inflation, and the economy of the nation took a downward trend. Ulysses S. Grant was elected president. Under Grant's presidency, the American people's confidence returned. Confidence returned when the president promised peace, prosperity, and security. Many Americans moved to the cities with more confidence, and the nation began to prosper again. The Industrial Revolution was beginning to mature, and there were jobs available for those who desired to work. The nation's culture (European) was maturing and becoming more sophisticated, but black people were kept from the means to provide for themselves and their families.

As previously mentioned, black people were uneducated and untrained. Those who managed to receive an education received an inferior education; they were poorly educated. Generally, many of them were not properly educated in order for them to take advantage of the opportunities presented by the Industrial Revolution. As a result, they moved to the slums of the cities and towns.

The nation underwent a sort of reconstruction process. During the Reconstruction, legislation gave rights to black citizens for the first time in the history of the United States. After the Reconstruction, black Americans gradually begin to gain grounds, although they still faced many difficulties along the way. There is hope that black America will eventually move up and take its rightful place in the American society in the not too distant future.

Black Americans were disenfranchised then, and they are now for the most part. They aren't on economic parity with their white counterparts. The reason behind this trend is apparent.

The Civil War is a classic indication that we aren't immune from turmoil here at home. We have had our share of turmoil in the past, and, God forbid, all indications suggested it was possibly for unrest to generate unruliness and lawlessness. Any and all threats that may be looming must be neutralized, whether they are from within or external. The problem of street gang activities, for example, is cause for concern. In addition, foreign drug cartels seem to target our nation and people for destruction. Our open border policy seems to be a magnet for illegal narcotic entry into this country, and this cannot be allowed to continue indefinitely.

Mexican drug lords are waging war, and it is spilling over into the USA. Unless we take corrective action to prevent these activities from breaching this nation, there is no telling what will happen next.

In connection with the history of this nation, a common thread between declined empires and the United States is identified. Is this nation declining? Will the United States lose its positions as super nation? With all that's happening in terms of various dilemmas, it's clear that stability is uncertain. And instabilities are getting the better of our nation and ourselves.

You have an understanding of the eyes of the universe. You are also aware of the law of rewards and punishment.

Above all, you are also aware of what is known as karma. With these dynamics in motion, there is no telling what the future holds for this nation.

Indications of America's Declining

The United States has reached its peak. It's failed to remain at the top and is descending. There are many indications to substantiate popular opinion around the globe and in this country that decline is taking place. I will look into elements that suggest the authenticity of the observation:

Percentage of Americans living below the poverty line, children living in poverty, income inequality, declining education, health care issues, prison population, etc. These are positive indicators suggesting that this nation is in trouble! In terms of social progress index (social well-being based on 52 economic indicators such as literacy, personal safety, etc) America is lagging far behind other developed nations.

There is work to be done if the United States should reverse this scourge and return to the plateau, and continue to be a superpower. Those that believed America is special (exceptional-ism) and that nothing should be done to make correction, will ensure that the USA will continue to become a second-rate power.

This chapter presented a fundamental and basic history of the early United States. I explained the concept of a republic as opposed to democracy. The arrival of the Europeans and the colonization of thirteen states were presented. The first congressional meeting and the Declaration of Independence were brought to your attention. In addition, elements that brought about war between the United States and Great Britain were also presented to you in the chapter. The Civil War and the Emancipation Proclamation that freed the slaves was explored.

JAMES A. HUDSON

What contributions have black Americans made to the development of the United States? A study of American history is not complete without a study of black American history.

Black American history will be addressed in the next chapter.

CHAPTER 7

Black Americans' Contribution To History

The United States has not been particularly kind to its black American citizens. The history of black Americans' contributions in the United States is almost always linked to slavery, emancipation, civil rights legislation, and so forth. These derogatory elements are all portrayed in a negative light. In truth and in fact, the authenticity of all of the above has been established. In reality, the African slaves were a stable part of the workforce in this country for more than two hundred years. Despite the negativity resulting from forced and freed labor, this nation became wealthy, prosperous, and powerful economically and militarily. There is no other way to interpret the phenomenon. The wealth and success of this nation is connected to the history of slavery and the aftermath of emancipation; black history is a part of the American history.

However, what is not well known to many is the history of black Americans, the descendants of the slaves, as they relate to true and substantial inventions and developments by early black people. Early black people invented and developed many gadgets for the good of this nation and the world. These things, unfortunately, aren't well known to the vast majority of Americans and others. In light of that fact, I will attempt to present historical information relative to the above-mentioned.

Injustice is one of the culprits that suppressed black people's inventions and kept their contributions under the rug. These injustices must be eliminated. Black people's contributions must be told. The breach must be repaired and take center stage in America. I dedicate this chapter to black American inventors and their inventions.

The emphasis is the things that black Americans have done in terms of making life easier for their fellow humans. These contributions made by early black inventors were enormous. It's a pity that the momentum did not continue by later black Americans.

African Americans' contributions to the development of the United States shouldn't be underestimated or forgotten. Early black people have done well, despite the oppression, discrimination, and segregation that were brought to bear upon them. Somehow, many of them managed to surmount the obstacles of oppression and invented many things to make life easier and pleasant not only for white America but for all people everywhere.

No, we aren't referring here to African Americans' athletic abilities or the musical talent that they have given the United States and the rest of the world. We are referring to real scientific and technological developments and inventions. Although many aren't aware of black Americans' achievements, many of their achievements are buried in the archives of US history for everyone to see.

I firmly believe these things should have been taught in school. They would undoubtedly generate interest by black people and instill confidence and optimism. They probably would motivate black Americans to continue inventing and developing for the good of this nation and its people.

Let's commence investigating black Americans' inventions, beginning with an invention by Alexander Mills.

The Elevator

What would the United States be today with buildings less than six stories high? You're probably saying that someone else would have invented the elevator. You may be correct.

Without the invention of the elevator, it would be virtually impossible to build multistory buildings. Skyscrapers would be impossible. Who would want to climb twelve floors of a building, much less ninety-nine floors or more? I certainly would not want to do that. Although there are many who are able to climb the staircase to third, fourth, and even fifth floors, the chronically ill would not be able to make it to the sixth floor and above.

Skyscrapers would be out of the question since the average person would not be able to make the trip up to the higher levels. To address this issue, a black person named Alexander Mills invented the elevator. With the invention of the elevator, we have been able to build tall and taller buildings.

Today's elevators are modern and complex. The humble beginning of this technology should never be forgotten.

Are you able to drive a motor vehicle? The answer is probably yes. Let me ask you another question. Are you able to drive a standard-transmission vehicle? A vehicle that has stick-shift transmission and a clutch? Many drivers cannot drive a manual transmission vehicle. Many have attested to the complication of driving such an automobile. The reason is automatic transmission does a far better job.

Automatic Transmission

The automobile is a wonderful invention indeed. Without it, the world would probably still be depending on the horse-drawn chariot. When the combustion engine was invented, the horse and buggy transportation was phased out, and the automobile was in. Then it was noted that it wasn't convenient for people to drive a manual transmission vehicle. The search began to find ways for the vehicle to change gears by itself, automatically. Richard Spike, a black person, came up with the final solution; he invented the automatic transmission as we know it today.

There is no fire in the belly to spark black Americans to carry on inventing. This has been lost over the centuries, and this is unfortunate. Worse, things that early black people invented have been taken over by major corporations. Black people are left out in the cold.

Supercharged System

Have you ever thought about the supercharged system for the internal combustion engine? This is another invention of a black person; Joseph Gammell's legacy is alive and well around the world today.

We have seen no indication that African Americans have invented destructive devices. Their inventions have made life less stressful in the home and office, even in driving our beloved automobiles. Black inventors have given men, women, and children the ability to get more done in less time, thus leaving them with more time to spend with loved ones, family, and friends. They should be commended for their contributions to America and the rest of the world.

The traffic signal control system that made it possible to control traffic at major and minor intersections was invented by a black person.

Traffic Signal Control System

Consider the traffic signals that control traffic automatically at intersections throughout the United States. Is this not a wonderful invention? Before the traffic signals were invented, police officers did the work of directing traffic in all kinds of weather. They were at the intersections from sunrise to sunset. They were there in the pouring rain, the snow, and the hail. Would it be safe and convenient for the police to be at intersections throughout the night, directing traffic? Probably not. The traffic signals were invented. A black person, Garrett A. Morgan, invented this gadget.

Electric trolleys that shuttle passengers throughout the cities and towns across the nation are another invention by a black person. In the first place, the trolley doesn't pollute the air. It's safe, reliable, and inexpensive. Trolleys are still a source of transportation in many cities today.

Electric Trolleys

Consider another invention by an early African American: the electric trolley. This is indispensable even to this day. Cities around the country found that trolleys are indispensable in terms of inexpensive transportation for people working and doing business in cities. One is able to park one's vehicle, take the trolley, and leave the driving to others. I found this concept convenient. If and when you park your vehicle and take a city trolley, you should remember Albert R. Morrison.

This form of urban/suburban transportation is still being used in many cities around the country to this day. Electric trolleys are propelled by electricity instead of combustion engines. Electric trolleys produce no pollution and are inexpensive to maintain. With the soaring price of oil, this nation is in dire need of more electric trolleys in every city and town. It would be an environmentally friendly way to curb our dependence on foreign oil.

Electric vehicles will be the wave of the future. Electricity can be derived from many sources: wind, sunlight (solar), and water (hydro). Turning to electricity for transportation is a good economical investment. The concept of an electric vehicle is not limited to trolleys. This invention is currently being used to power motor vehicles as well.

Street Sweepers

Have you ever considered the fact that men and women once pushed brooms to sweep our streets on a daily basis? This was long before the invention of the motorized street sweeper. Yes, they did. These workers were called "sanitary engineers" to bring some dignity into the low-level work they were engaged in. These people rose early in the mornings, went to the city yard, picked up their brooms and other necessities, and went off to the streets they were assigned to clean. At daybreak, citizens found their streets clean and free of litter. This was a normal routine for street sweepers until the invention of the mechanical street sweeper.

No work is degrading—and rightfully so—but sweeping streets wasn't a task that was uplifting. It was downright degrading and demeaning to those involved. This was degrading then and still would be today. Fortunately, someone came up with the idea to invent a machine that would do the filthy work for humans.

The inventor of the mechanical street sweeper was probably a street sweeper or may have had a connection with someone engaged in that sort of job. Charles Brooke came up with the idea of a mechanical street sweeper.

African American contributions to the development of the United States should never be denied or swept under the carpet. Instead, this nation should be grateful and proud of the good things that they have done. Black history month should be national and incorporate white people and others. It should bring to light the contributions of these people, which include the contingents of slaves that were engaged in the construction of the White House, the United States Capitol, and national monuments.

Who invented the air conditioner and the refrigerator? One would be surprised to know that these things were invented by black people. Before the invention of this equipment, things were very bad. The absence of the above inventions appeared to be normal in those days.

Air Conditioner

The American people are aware of the importance of air-conditioning and heating systems. This invention has far-reaching implications on the lives of men, women, and children. How would American society function today without air-conditioning technology? It probably could since it once existed without it.

Electric fans were available and still are, but they are no match for an AC system. Modern science has refined air-conditioning technology for more efficient cooling in homes and offices and in commerce and industry. In addition, air-conditioning units can be found in marine vehicles, automobiles, and aircraft. The importance of the air conditioner cannot be underestimated.

Who invented the air conditioner? If you said it was Thomas Edison, you would be wrong. It was Fredrick Jones's invention. Jones was an African American. Jones gave the world the air conditioner and the refrigerator. They shared similar technology. These two creature comforts are standard amenities and are essential today.

Black people aren't dumb—as society would have us believe. Give them the necessary education and training, and they will do marvelous things.

Refrigerators and Coolers

Air conditioners and refrigerators are two important inventions. How would a modern society function without them? Let's take the refrigerator for example. People who are living in temperate regions may or may not need to use an air conditioner. A refrigerator may be essential in temperate zones and tropical regions. It makes their lives more pleasant and convenient. The invention of the refrigerator was a good one. Before the refrigerator was invented, it was customary to use an icebox to store food and water. Ice was made in commercial plants and trucked to homes, offices, and businesses. With the invention of the refrigerator, this practice quickly changed. There was no need for an ice truck to transport ice to homes, offices, and businesses. One simply purchased a refrigerator to take care of the business of refrigeration.

John Standard, an African American, invented the refrigerator. John, we salute you for giving us this creature comfort that plays an indispensable role in the lives of everyone.

This brings us to the heating furnace, an indispensable appliance of today.

Furnaces

Heating a house and other enclosures in the winter was dangerous business. Any attempt to heat an enclosure without strictly adhering to the laws of physics, chemistry, and common sense often resulted in disaster. Many people lost their lives from carbon monoxide poisoning over the years due to toxic fumes. Care must be taken to prevent dangerous fumes from building up in an enclosure that is heated by any form of gas, oil, or coal. Another genius came up with the invention of the heating furnace. A furnace is a safe and efficient way to control enclosed heat. Alice Parker, an African American woman, invented this type of heating equipment.

Alice Parker's vision for controlling heat in a dwelling is probably the best thing ever. Today, there are many versions of the heating furnace, which ranges from automatic electronic controls to manually controlled versions. Alice Parker took the prize in the heating business. For this, we are more than grateful to you, Alice. Black men weren't the only inventors; black women were also inventors.

Clothes-Drying Equipment

Isn't it nice to be able to throw a bunch of wet clothes into a machine that will dry them without catching the house on fire? This would be convenient, wouldn't it? Such a machine is available, and it is the clothes dryer. A clothes dryer is convenient, especially to those who are restricted by time and space.

Hanging clothes on the back or front porch or even stretching wires across lawns are things of the past for the most part. There are people today who still engage in the practice of hanging clothes on lines in the summertime in order to reduce utility bills. In any case, the electric and gas dryers are convenient machines in almost every house in the United States today. Credit should go to George T. Samon, an African American, for this invention.

Modern clothes-drying equipment has gone high-tech in domestic and commercial outlets. Again, credit should be given where credit is due.

These helpful inventions by black Americans might never have been born without the creative ingenuity of each person involved. Everyone is born with special talent or gift to benefit the human race. The next time you toss your clothes into the dryer, whether it is gas or electric, take a second to thank George T. Samon for this time-saving necessity.

How about the shoes that you wear on your feet? Are they a good invention or what?

Inventing shoes and the machines to produce them are two different things. Jan may not be the invention of the shoe, but he certainly is the inventor of the shoe lasting machine.

Shoe Lasting Machine

Have you ever considered the importance of the shoe lasting machine? This invention by an African American brought to an end the painstaking manual method of making shoes. Jan Matzeliger believed there had to be a way to mass produce shoes for home consumption and for export. Matzeliger invented this machine to mass produce shoes for the domestic market and to export to other nations. We should never forget the contributions these people have made to the advancement of our nation and the world. These things may not be superior inventions by many people, but they have contributed to a better way of life for all in terms of comfort, convenience, and efficiency.

Then came another invention for a convenient way of writing. The fountain pen brought an end to the old method of using feathers for writing.

JAMES A. HUDSON

The Fountain Pen

The basic fountain pen led to the modern ballpoint pen, which is still important. Fountain pens are still being used today; in fact, old fountain pens are regarded as treasures and can cost a fortune, especially gold-plated ones. Fountain pens are unique in that they contain ink in a tubular arrangement in the center of the pen. The tubular arrangement is made of soft rubber or a thin metal strip and rubber combination that is rolled into a kind of cylindrical form. The ink container can be filled with ink by squeezing the rubber or rubber and plastic arrangement.

This is accomplished by squeezing a prescribed area of the pen's body to create suction, allowing the ink to be sucked into the tank of the fountain pen. The pouch, when filled with ink, is able to write until the ink is finished. When it is replenished, it is ready for another task. The throwaway concept as it applies to the modern ballpoint pen was not necessary. Fountain pens can be used and reused indefinitely. It's only necessary to replace the part that makes contact with the paper in the process of writing.

Before fountain pens were invented, feathers were the standard writing instrument. Reeds and branches were also used.

The ballpoint pen is a descendant of the old fountain pen. The fountain pen is the forerunner of the modern ballpoint pen. The ballpoint pen was invented by William Purvis, an African American. Unfortunately, black people receive little or no credit and recognition for their contributions. Many have tried to hijack their inventions by claiming them to be their own, including the invention of the printing press.

The Printing Press

What would the printing industry do without the invention of high-speed printing? They would not be able to print newspapers, books, magazines, and a host of other things at very high speeds we know today. Printing has come a long way from the days of the old manual presses that were slower than old computer line printer. In any event, manual printing presses were done away with when Alex Lovette invented the rapid printing press.

Today, with the advent of electronics technology, the printing industry has no limits on its ability to print in black and white and in many colors.

Black Americans' inventions truly have made life more pleasant. These inventions allowed men and women to have more time to spend with family in the United States and overseas I will not continue with the long list of inventions by African Americans. In addition to these inventions, you can add the lawnmower, the lawn sprinkler system, paint, and postal boxes.

The fact that should be emphasized here is that credit should be given where credit is due. It's my duty to focus the spotlight on this group of people for their contributions to the development of the United States and the world.

Before we bring this topic to a close, there are two important inventions by black Americans that you should be mindful of. They are the telephone and the electric light bulb.

Before we bring you the history of the electric lamp, you should be aware that it was Lewis Latimer, an African American, whose work made it possible for Alexander Graham Bell to patent and develop the telephone. Hail to Lewis Latimer for assisting Alexander Graham Bell in patenting the telephone.

Lewis Latimer was born in Chelsea, Massachusetts, in 1848 to George and Rebecca Latimer, an escaped slave from Virginia. Lewis Latimer enlisted in the Union Navy at the age of fifteen by forging the age on his birth certificate. Upon the completion of his military service, Latimer returned to Boston where he was employed by the solicitors Crosby & Gould. While working in the law office, Lewis studied drawing and eventually became the head of the drafting department.

During his employment with this law firm, Latimer drafted the patented drawings for Alexander Graham Bell's application for the telephone. He spent long nights and days with Bell developing the drawing for the telephone. The drawing was eventually completed, and Bell rushed his patent application to the patent office just ahead of the competition. He won the patent right to the telephone with the help and assistance of Lewis Latimer. Thus, the telephone was born.

With the aid of technology, there are many versions of the telephone today. Telephone technology has come a long way since Alexander Graham Bell—thanks to Lewis Latimer's involvement. This resulted in the invention and development of telephone technology.

This was not his only invention. Larimore singlehandedly invented electric bulbs.

The Electric Light Bulb

What would the world be without electric light? Someone else probably would have invented the electric light bulb, but Larimer invented it first. Naturally, this is something to think about.

Hail to Lewis Latimer for inventing the electric lamp. Lewis Latimer was an assistant manager and draftsman at the electric company of H. R. Maxim in Bridgeport, Connecticut. Latimer's talent for drawing and his creative genius led him to invent a method of making carbon filaments for the maxim incandescent electric bulb. This invention made possible the birth of the electric lamp as we know it today.

In 1881, Latimer supervised the installation of electric lighting in New York City, Philadelphia, Montreal, Canada, and London, England.

Mr. Latimer was the original draftsman for Thomas Edison. Latimer was the only African American member of the twenty-four "Edison Pioneers," Thomas Edison's engineering division of the Edison Company.

Latimer went on to coauthor a book on electricity. *Incandescent Electric Lighting* was published in 1890. This book is still in print and can be obtained in the circle of literature dealing with the science of electricity. Latimer was truly a genius. He was an inventor, draftsman, engineer, author, poet, and musician. Notwithstanding his commitment and contributions to science and technology, he was also a devoted family man and a philanthropist.

Black people are capable of doing great things, similar to any other race. People may be born with gifts and talents, however, they must be developed through education and training.

This chapter highlighted the inventions and developments that black people have contributed to the advancement of the United States and the world. Unfortunately, the will and desire of contemporary black Americans to move ahead and continue the legacy of their former counterparts, in terms of invention and development, seems to no longer exist. At the same time, this nation is in desperate need of inventors and developers. There is no need for black people to be lagging behind.

An education is the missing link that stands in the way of black Americans. Although there are black people who reached great heights in the field of education, others are lagging behind. The declining of inner-city decay continues.

Student loans are available and should be use when necessary. In addition, those who served in the military are entitled to receive educational training under the GI Bill, which is available for that purpose. It's time for black Americans to come of age economically, socially, and politically. White Americans have a duty and responsibility to assist black Americans in gaining economic parity. Are the old guards still at their posts and preventing black Americans from rising? If this is the case, then there is a problem.

This chapter presented the inventions of early black American. As you have seen, they have made significance contributions to this nation as enslaved people and as freed people. Slaves have never been compensated for their forced labor. Worst of all, their generation has never received reparations for the contributions of their ancestors. Instead, these people are treated as outcasts. Racism, discrimination, and exclusion are brought to bear on them. In a single word, they were subjected to *injustice*.

The eyes and ears of the universe have these things in their memory. Sooner or later, justice will be rendered. It would be wise if the powers that be would make a concerted effort to level the playing field before time runs out.

Black American Society

A study of the history of the United States could not be completed without the history of black Americans. Black people play an important part of the history of this country. It's unfortunate that back Americans have not come of age economically, socially, and politically in this country in 2020. There are wealthy and middle-class black Americans, but these classes of people are few and far between. Those at the lower levels, which are the overwhelming number of black people, should be helped up the ladder of success. Until black people at the lower economic levels are lifted up, black society will have little to be proud about. Poverty has no place in this country. We are too rich, too advanced, and too respected from a military standpoint to tolerate poverty, ignorance, and lawlessness.

Why aren't rich black people, middle-class black people, and black intellectuals not coming to the rescue of poverty-stricken inner-city black people? Worse, why isn't there a pipeline instituted by them to bring motivational assistance to black people who are at a disadvantage?

At the same time, the problem of black fathers' delinquency is taking its toll. The cycle of crime, violence, and poverty continues. I don't like the popular opinion about young inner-city black men. I often overhear people say, "Some of those so-called basketball stars are big, tall, and fast, but many of them are as dumb as a doornail."

Many critics are referring to an incident propagated by three black Americans who went to China to take part in sports. Unfortunately, these young men were charged with shoplifting. Naturally, these things are scars on black American society. These young men need mentoring. Again, where are the black people intellectuals? Why isn't there a communication link between all American black people? These things are necessary, and other races in this country have such a link between their people. These things are essential.

In this chapter, we have presented relevant information based on history. We bring proof that black people were far more advanced than contemporary black people. The problems of inner-city black people were addressed. Well-off black people should come to the assistance of other black people. Unless black people at the poverty line are lifted out of poverty, black Americans will not come of age in this country. I am calling on black Americans who are affluent—and those who are intellectually capable—to come to the assistance of their people who are lagging behind.

The ruling class and the elites believe that the masses are naive. Frankly, they presented evidence to prove their point. As a result, we will turn these things around by bringing motivational assistance to those who lagging behind. We will turn around the notion that the public is dumb and naive in the next chapter.

CHAPTER 8

Motivational Assistance to the Left Behind

This message to the masses is intended to bring awareness to Americans who are lagging behind in terms of prosperity, skills, and opportunity. This applies to those who are permanently residing in this country and find themselves at the bottom of the economic ladder. This relevant information has been carefully designed and integrated to bring harmony instead of friction, togetherness instead of isolation, and prosperity instead of lack and poverty. There are many races, nationalities, and cultures living together in America. We must all get along. There must be some common elements that bind us together. If this isn't the case, then America and Americans will be in constant turmoil. Unfortunately, this currently is the case in this country, and this is intolerable. If fact, these things are contributing to the downing of the United States. Poverty is the breeding ground for crime and violence. And heaven knows, the scourge of crime and violence knows no boundary in this country.

To compound the above, internal strife, political unrest, voice, and retributions are taking their toll in the United States. These things are eroding the United States' ability to lead as a superpower. These dynamics are factors that cannot be allowed to continue. I am calling on Americans of both major political parties, and others, to put their differences aside and work toward unity, success, peace, and prosperity for the common good of all. Selfishness, greed, retribution, and hatred are negative elements that are wrecking this nation.

The fact is, America has reached its peak, failed to remain at the summit, and it's descending. Meanwhile, Red China will be on par with America within twenty years. And within forty years it will undoubtedly overtake and become the next superpower nation.

Due to lack of education and the scourge of ignorance and poverty, the ruling class, the elite, believe the masses are naïve and dumb. They have cited many reasons for this disparagement. I will bring some of them to your attention in this chapter. First, let's focus on the pressing issues facing urban people and people living in rural areas who are at and below the poverty line. These are some of the people who need to be lifted up the ladder of success.

The fact is that in a capitalistic society, keeping the masses in ignorance and in darkness are advantageous to the ruling class! They are easily led by politicians, and others who are able to con them and influence them as they will.

Urban Populations

Inner-city people in America are almost always black people, Hispanic people, or white people who are not economically well off. These are some of the people who are at an economic disadvantage. We will bring strategies to their attention to lift them up the ladder of success. For these people to be lifted out of the dilemmas of poverty, some fundamental requirements must be met. One of them is an education. The next requirement is marketable skills. There are other requirements such as appearance, mannerism, sobriety etc. We will look into these issues as we continue.

In terms of appearance, it should be understood by everyone that a neat and pleasing appearance will generate people's confidence and trust. Due to diverse cultures and customs, there are those living in this culture whose appearances and attire often clash with the American way of life. These people can readily be identified right away. These are some of the dynamics working in this country.

Black and Hispanic people in cities believe they are at an economic disadvantage. In addition, many black people believe they are victims of circumstance. In truth and in fact, they aren't victims of circumstance. This will become clear to them during this presentation. The question of disadvantage is another matter. Many of these people are at a disadvantage, but they are at a disadvantage because they have failed to qualify themselves in order to take advantage of existing and future opportunities. I will point them in the right direction for success.

First, it should be clear that preparation is the key. One cannot hope to go on a long journey without being prepared. If one intended to drive from New York to Los Angeles, the first line of thinking would have to be planning the drive. It may be necessary to consult a map for driving direction beforehand. There is no point in leaving New York without knowing the directions to California. This would be confusing, wouldn't it? Similar principles can be applied to success. One will not achieve any lasting success without preparation.

Let's consider black Americans since they make up almost 13 percent of the American population.

Black America

In America, black society is divided into three components: rich, middle class, and poor. It's not surprising then that those at the lower level of black society are at a disadvantage. I place the emphasis on disadvantage rather than victimhood as many may believe. This disadvantage is brought about by the failure of government and the failure of black people. Many of them aren't prepared for success. Am I wrong about this?

Before we continue, it should be clear that America is responsible for the economic disparities between the rich and the poor. The legacy of discrimination and bigotry plays an important part in this dynamic. The passage of time hasn't lessened this to any extent. Actually, there are steps that Americans of good will are taking to bring about changes in this area.

There are underlying problems and other problems for inner-city black men in this country. Education and training are some of the keys to success. Unfortunately, with a criminal record, one may not be qualified for student loans for college. More often than not, many of those with criminal records will not be able to qualify for good-paying jobs. In many cases, these people are doomed to living at the poverty line or below it.

It's clear that a nation will not advance when a segment of its people is in poverty. The United States is an advanced and wealthy nation. However, we are lagging behind many industrial nations in educating our people and race relations. These issues must be cured before America can heal. Frankly, there is lots of healing to be done. What is of concern to us in this book, though, is the advancement of the masses, the general public. This includes Americans of all races, colors, and national origins.

In this case, the family structure would be the appropriate place to direct these instructions. Due to the breakdown of the family unit, especially in many inner-cities, I have decided to write to young black people, Latino people, poor white people, and other nationalities in this country. This doesn't necessarily mean that parents and guardians are exempt. They are encouraged to lead the way to a brighter future for the next generation of Americans. This also applies to white people at the lower end of the economic spectrum since a rising tide will raise all vessels.

The ruling class believes the masses are bums. At this time, it's necessary to bring attention to the reasons behind this observation by the ruling class.

Black Friday Sales

There are people who will camp out overnight in parking lots with the intention of going to the head of the line for Black Friday sales. During the process, fighting results between people competing for similar gadgetry. These actions aren't something one should be proud of. These actions cross racial and ethnic lines. White people, black people, and Hispanics people are equally to blame for these things. Hanging out in a parking lot overnight to be first in line at any sale is ridiculous. This is one of the reasons cited by those at the top, but that is not all. Whenever a new electronic gadget hits the store, there seems to be a frenzy to own the product. Many of these people will storm the place to be first in line. These people will pay any amount to get their hands on the latest iPhone, smart-phone, X box, or TV. These are some of the things I intend to bring to light. I could have gone on and on, but this will suffice to bring attention to the relevant information.

With all due respect, the ruling class has reasons to believe the masses are naive. We all want to save money and look forward to sales at department stores. Nevertheless, camping out in parking lots overnight isn't worth the trouble.

I want to stress the importance of education. On an individual basis, no one will gain economic independence without plans and investments in the future. One of the ways to go about this is through the acquisition of knowledge. Knowledge is an important key. Hitting the lottery jackpot and not being knowledgeable about how to deal with wealth will be disadvantageous to the winner. The money will soon depart due to that lack of knowledge: "The fool and his money will soon part, but wisdom, knowledge, and understanding will abide forever."

When I refer to education, I'm not referring to those who are affluent and are able to send their children to institutions of higher learning. We are not concerned here about professions or professional people in this presentation. I am referring to young people who are at the poverty line. They should have been through the school system, graduated from high school, and attended at least a technical school or community colleges. These are important, and anyone who fails to realize these things is missing the boat completely.

There are many technical skills to choose from. I will not attempt to list them all here. Selecting a skill is an individual choice. One may prefer to become an electrician, an electronics technician, or an auto mechanic, or welder. This nation is in need of skill craft men/women!

Whatever skills one would like to pursue, it's clear that one must pass through the various stages of the educational process. Please note that our country needs skilled workers. You owe it to yourself and to your family—or your prospective family—to prepare for the future. Digging ditches may be honorable, but you can do better than that. This is not to say that something is wrong with digging ditch, or mowing grass to make quick money. However, a long-term plan should be in place to learn a skill.

Engaging in manual, unskilled tasks should be a means to an end. One can engage in a ditch-digging task, pushing brooms, or things of that nature with the aim in mind to accumulate enough money to go to school and acquire a skill. This is perfectly understandable and totally acceptable. Skilled workers command reasonable salaries in comparison to those who are engaging in manual tasks.

Knowledge is the way to lift oneself out of poverty. Unfortunately, many who are at and below the poverty line are not prepared for the future. It may not have been their fault then. It may have been a lack of guidance. Whatever the case may have been, you can start over again—right at this moment. We will show you the ways to success if you have the will and desire to succeed. If you use this information to the best of your ability, you will soon start making progress for the future and toward happiness.

Message to Urban and Rural Populations

The message here is very clear, straightforward, and to the point. Since radical changes are necessary, mincing words or disguising facts is out of the question. The truth must be told to many urban and rural people at the poverty line. As promised, I will bring attention to the correct paths you should take. I'm not condemning or disparaging those of you who found yourselves in situations where you feel hopeless. There is hope. From this point onward, you will be given hope and inspiration. You should strive to forge ahead to a brighter future. You will be in a position to strive and not merely getting by day by day.

Here are three things you should be aware of: educate yourself as much as you can, invest positively in the future, and stop considering yourself a victim of circumstances.

We will analyze these statements to determine their relevancy in the grand scheme of things. Most problems facing young people in urban and rural areas at the poverty level can be traced to the absence of one or more of these suggestions. Some of the paralysis that is afflicting them is self-inflicted, and others are government failures. In any event, young people must lift themselves up by the bootstraps and move on to gain economic prosperity.

Please let's examine the third suggestion: stop being victim of circumstances. This often applies to many at the lower level of black American society.

Stop Being a Victim of Circumstances

To stop being victims of circumstances is the factor I will analyze first. There is no member of the black community in this country who is a victim of circumstances in terms of a lack of opportunities. Opportunities are there. There are opportunities all over this nation for black people and other people. Many have failed to grasp these opportunities because of failure. They aren't prepared in the first place. This places them at a disadvantage.

Why is it that so many foreign nationals are granted permission to come and work in the United States? There is a shortage of skilled Americans. This includes black people, white people, Hispanic people, and others. My concern here is related to young black men in some cases since men are supposed to be the heads of their families. The burden is on men more than women regardless of race. Unfortunately, many inner-city black women are the main providers for their families. The reason behind the dilemma should be apparent to everyone in this country.

Black Americans, please understand that your ancestors were the victims. They were the ones who were oppressed, victimized, and forced to labor without reward. They weren't given reparations for their contributions to American society. Nevertheless, black people in the United States today, especially those whose ancestors were enslaved in America, are victors.

Black people do have equal rights and justice under the prevailing laws of this country. In the recent past, this was not the case. There is no limitation as far as opportunities for black people are concerned. The only limitations are the limitations that one places on oneself. The educational system leaves much to be desired, but black people are able to attend school if they so desire. Besides, it is free from the elementary level up to high school.

For technical high schools, colleges, and universities, student loans are available. If you aren't a convict, the chance of getting a student loan is very good. There is a catch. Student loans must be repaid.

As far as black Americans are concerned, I believe that black students should be exempt from repayment of government student loans. This should be a form of reparation in connection with your ancestors, ex-slaves, and slavery. I am suggesting that the victim mentality needs to go. They should pick themselves up and make something of themselves. If you are one of these people, I invite you to modify your ways of thinking.

This victim mentality is like crying wolf. If black people are qualified, they will be able to be successful. They will be able to complete. There will be no need for the government to grant work visas and work permits to foreign workers. Many are coming in and taking advantage of good-paying job opportunities. There is an urgent need for professionals and semiprofessionals in this country. Due to a shortage of qualified Americans, the government has no choice but to grant permission to those from foreign nations to do the jobs that young Americans and others aren't qualified to do.

In my opinion, America should be exporting skills, scientists, engineers, and technicians all over the globe. Instead, we are actually inviting these people to come in and help us since we aren't producing the talented people that are needed. These things are eroding the ability of America to remain a superpower.

Black, white, and Latino people in this country need to produce more professionals at all levels. This is especially true for minorities. Too many young black people and Latinos in the inner cities are lagging behind when they should stand up and be counted. This is to the disadvantage of everyone in black and Latino society. These young men and women need direction.

Failure Is All Around

Wealthy and intellectual minorities aren't doing squat, zilch, zero about lifting up their people. Am I right about this? I stand to be corrected, however, as far as I know, this is the case. African Americans don't help their own to climb the ladder of success. Those who are economically well off moved to higher grounds, which is unfortunate. What has happened to our rich and middle-class black American people? In addition, what has happened to black intellectuals? What has happened to the leaders of the civil rights movement? What plan do they have to turn the tide that is working against young black men, and others, in inner cities across this nation? They should launch an organization with the intention to elevate blacks and others who are lagging behind. This proposed mentoring association would see to it that Blacks, Latinos, Whites, and others at the poverty line are brought up in an appropriate manner, receive a quality education, gain at least one marketable skill, and are upright and productive citizens.

Self-control, discipline, and tolerance are qualities that are lacking in this country. The younger generation is void of discipline, and this is unfortunate. We need to educate the younger generation so that they will be able to carry on when we, the current generation, are gone.

There are many wealthy black people in the United States. Why can't wealthy black people launch a banking system to grant loans to black people who are willing to start a business? They should grant interest-free loans to members of their race who want to start businesses in cities or towns. Where they are? Wouldn't the idea be plausible?

In any gas station, convenience store, and beauty salon etc, in America, who will be at the counter? They are almost always foreigners. Foreigners come in, see the opportunities, and make use of them. Black people at lower economic levels don't have the money to invest in business. They received no assistance from their affluent brothers and sisters who are basking in wealth.

Meanwhile, these foreigners are on the fast track to becoming wealthy, and some people in the inner city are planning to rob them of their possessions. They should be advised that they are unwittingly bringing 'misfortune' on themselves when they rob, hurt, or take the lives of others. They will never prosper in this life.

In terms of transportation, when is the last time you saw a black taxi driver or taxi fleet owner in a major metropolitan area? You talk about foreign accents? Many taxi drivers cannot even speak the American version of English. These jobs should have been held by young black and white Americans. Instead, black people are playing the victim and playing the racism card as much as possible.

These dilemmas in black American society will not go away until substantial social, economic, and political, progress is made. Let's teach our young black men, and others in the inner cities and rural areas, how to be men. How can the black American society hope to come of age when the next generation is stagnant, lagging behind, semiliterate, undisciplined, and unskilled? These are some of the scourge on this nation that's contributing to its decline. Action is needed now. Therefore, I am calling on black America to wake up and give a helping hand to people who are in economic distress. Help them rise up the ladder of success that you have ridden to the top.

Let's move on to the next part of the message in this process—education—since this is an important part of financial freedom and prosperity. Let's contemplate the importance of an educated mind, body, and soul, as opposed to ignorance and lack of information. Education and training are important elements in the lives of all Americans. Although the ruling class and the elite would rather the masses remain ignorant, it's their responsibility to lift themselves up by the bootstraps.

Educate Yourself

I have written many books dedicated to bring motivational assistance to those who are left behind, those who needed to be lifted out of poverty. I received no help from the news media in bringing them to the attention of inner-city people, and those in rural areas. I also contacted officials in the African Americans society, but to no avail. In addition, I also reached out to officials of the Democratic Party since Africans Americans seems to show some form of allegiance to that Party. They didn't respond to me as well. By the way, isn't the Democrat Party the Party of slavery, segregation, Jim Crow, and the KKK? If the answer to any of the above is positive, why would the Africans Americans support such party? The question is, are they aware of the history in connection with these things?

Let's not be mistaken, there are wealthy black Americans. Nevertheless, it should be noted that if the black Americans people should gain the respect they rightfully deserve, they should unite and help each other, instead of division and voice between themselves.

And so, the importance of an educated mind is the next item in connection with this message. Education is a lifelong process. Passing through the educational process is only the beginning on the long road through life. One never stops learning. This is a fact. One should open one's mind to learning new things at all times, and there are many things to be learned in life. No matter the level of education, people should learn something new on a daily basis. Life is a learning process, and this will continue for as long as we all live.

Older people realize there are many things still to be learned. People can learn through newspapers, television newscasts, and radio newscasts. Any of these are rich sources of local, national, and international information.

First and foremost, one should be informed about what's happening in local cities and towns. In addition, what is transpiring across the nation should not be ignored. Unfortunately, there are many people who do not know the name of the mayor in the city in which they live. It may not be convenient for many people to read a daily newspaper. In this case, local radio and television newscasts will bring news to inform them about local and national developments. The news is a great source of information for what is transpiring across the nation, including international matters.

Entertainment has its place. Nevertheless, education and skills training should take precedence over entertainment. There are those who will watch entertainment television 24/7 instead of picking up a book. Others will find other trivialities to engage in instead of doing constructive things to their benefit and the benefit of their loved ones. The world is made up of all sorts of people. Fortunately, people can be identified by their words, thoughts, and deeds. People can also be identified by the programs they watch on television. People can be identified by what they do and what they fail to do.

Another element to be considered in the equation, according to the ruling class, is that the masses are uninformed. They are poorly informed since they lack knowledge. They are easily manipulated, and they often fall victim to all sorts of deceptions. They believe these people cannot think for themselves. God forbid this is the case when it comes to politics in this country. Some of these people will believe anything they are told by politicians or salesmen. These things are unfortunate.

If you are one of these people, you are encouraged to be proactive in terms of gathering information. This will give one's a bird-eye's view of things that are happening in this nation and around the world.

In addition to the above, it's a good idea to visit your local library. At your local library, you will find a wealth of information. It is not only found in books. These days, there are books on tape and compact discs. One can learn many things by reading books or listening to taped information. There are thousands of valuable pieces of information in libraries. It takes discipline and determination to improved one's self by gathering information, but your efforts will pay off in due time.

We should never forget that the future of this nation, the United States, rests squarely on the next generation of Americans. I strongly suggest that academics should be given priority over sports and other trivialities. Is the next generation of Americans fully qualified and ready to take charge of this nation? If not, should America look to foreign citizens to come in and administer the affairs of this nation? I hope not. Preparation is the key for the future of this nation and its people if we want to remain a superpower.

Enlightenment also comes from deep within your being. This means you should take time to get to know yourself. Listen to your inner voice. Here is the way in which you should go about the process. Put away all distraction and disturbances: TV, telephone, computer, everything. Take a little time to be alone and be still. Now, be silent and listen to what is going on inside you. If you haven't done this before, that's okay. We live, and we learn. Now, can you hear the beating of your heart? If you are able to hear the beating of your heart, you are on the right path to hearing your inner voice. If not, repeat the process at different times until you do. Whenever the opportunity arises, repeat the process until you make progress. This exercise will allow you to tune in to yourself.

Your Soul Needs Your Attention

For those who are not religiously inclined, you should bear in mind that people are threefold beings. I brought this to your attention earlier. Let's repeat this again because of its importance. People consist of a body, a mind, and a soul. If you are a religious person, you should have known this already. If you aren't, now is the time to learn. Whatever you do, you should understand that the soul has all the answers to your problems. The soul is a part of God. The difficult part is making contact with your inner soul or spirit. Please get acquainted with your inner self and begin to bring about the necessary changes in your life.

Silence is golden. Do not be afraid to go in silence and concentrate with yourself on a regular basis. Noise and other excitement are distractions to your soul; this can prevent prosperity, inner peace, and tranquility. Prosperity can only be achieved through preparation and with a clear mind, a calm spirit, and true inner peace. You must set aside time to be in tune with your inner self. "Stop your fighting—and know that I am God, exalted among the nations, exalted on the earth" (Psalm 46:10).

People are partners with God. Many people may be skeptical about this fact. As a result, please see proof here: "The Lord of Host is with us; the God of Jacob is our stronghold" (Psalm 46:11).

And now, let's move on to the next instruction: invest positively for the future. There is a very good reason for saving this second instruction in this series for now. This will be apparent as we continue in the process.

Invest Positively in the Future

A positive investment in the future is something that everyone is working to accomplish—or should have been working to accomplish. Investing positively in the future is the purpose behind an education and the acquisition of skills. This is the reason parents and guardians send children to school. The responsibility of parents and guardians legally ends at the age of eighteen or twenty-one, depending on the state in which you are living. If the child wasn't exposed to the educational process, the child will be at a disadvantage. Young adults are responsible for themselves from then on. This is not to say that parents do not have a moral responsibility to the child after the child has reached the legal age of adulthood. In any event, from a legal perspective, their responsibility is terminated. The child, in all probability, must carve out their own future and destiny.

If the young adult happens to be educated before leaving their parents' home, they probably have marketable skills, a profession, or some other meaningful way to earn a living. Young adults should be able to provide for themselves and their connections. They may fall in love and get married or consider doing so. A wise young adult will make positive contributions in the future. The future is the thing we will be discussing as we continue.

If the child wasn't exposed to an education or an adequate education and doesn't have marketable, what will be their future? This person may be illiterate. This person will probably need educational assistance and marketable skills. Many Americans have found themselves in this situation. This program is designed for people in similar dilemmas.

Here is a startling reminder that we will not remain young forever. That preparation for the future is the key. The cycle from birth to death is relatively short—under a hundred years.

The Days of Your Life

Every adult has approximately forty-five working years in life. They work to take care of their families and themselves and to prepare for retirement, old age, and death. After retirement, between the ages of sixty-five and seventy, it is said to be downhill. As a result, time is relatively short in terms of the allotted time given to people.

The years of our lives are "three score years and ten," but by reason of good health and strength, it's possible to outlive the appointed time. Twenty times three plus ten gives us a grand total of seventy years. This is the allotted time for people. Living past the age of seventy is "living on borrowed time." Some people have lived to be ninety or even one hundred. Some of these people are in relatively good health, and others aren't. We should endeavor to seek wisdom, knowledge, and understanding. This should be clear in your mind from now on.

Too many Americans have ended up on the streets when they have reached the ripe old age of retirement. Many have ended up on the street well before the age of seventy, and this is unfortunate. I cannot overstretch the importance of preparation. It's clear that too many young Americans are wasting precious time on trivial pursuits instead of trying to make a decent living for themselves and their connections.

America is a wealthy nation, but poverty is entrenched in this society. Poverty is the root of crime and violence for the most part. It should never be forgotten that hungry people are angry people. Poverty brings crimes and all the negative dynamics that go along with it. Crime is rampant in this country; there is no question about that.

Let me remind you again of important providential instructions. Below you will see portions of the Ten Commandments. I encourage everyone to adhere to them while the sun is still shining on the land of the living.

Thou shall not steal, and thou shall not kill. The law in this country also forbids stealing and killing. The difference is that if someone happens to steal or kill and isn't caught, they will probably go free. This is not the case when it comes to the all-seeing eyes of the universe. No one can escape the all-seeing eyes of God. Those who are guilty of any of the above crimes will pay today or tomorrow. They will pay beyond the grave.

A prayer from an ancient order has been around for thousands of years. I will not reveal the name of the order, but it is still functioning to this day. Branches of the order can be found in many civilized nations across the globe: "Almighty God, maker of the Universe, we return Thee sincere thanks for all favors received at Thy hand, and mayest thou impress upon every brothers' heart that, wherever we are and whatever we do, Thine all-seeing eyes behold us."

I reveal this to make an important point: one may fool oneself or others, but no one can fool Providence. It should be clear to everyone that one may evade the laws of people, but no one can evade the laws of the all-seeing eyes of an offended God. Therefore, to those who are bent on committing crime and violence, please stop and turn yourself around. Do not continue to bring destruction upon yourself, your race, and your family. It may be tempting to take something that doesn't belongs to you. This is due to poverty in most cases. Nevertheless, you should think about the shame and disgrace that often follows. One should think of the dilemma of being arrested and thrown in jail. You should think of the consequences of any action. Plunging headlong into doing things without carefully considering the consequences is the prescription of fools.

I have presented several main points in this chapter. Other messages of importance will be given soon. We have discussed five principles for success. I promised to go into them in detail in terms of analyzing them for further clarification. Therefore, let's continue the process to determine their relevance in the scheme of things.

Definitions

We have presented five principles for success. These principles are important in the lives of the masses. I invite those at the lower economic level to pay attention, make corrections, and govern themselves accordingly.

Principle 1: A Formal Education Is Essential for Success

This means that one should go to school. A child should not quit school before graduation. Dropping out of school for whatever reason will have negative consequences on the individual throughout life. The objective should be to complete high school and not drop out. After completing high school, one should learn at least one marketable skill. To acquire marketable skills, one could attend community college or a technical school. There are many such institutions to choose from; the choice is up to the individual.

Those who possess the necessary aptitude may continue to an institution of higher learning. There are many ways to acquire success, and educating oneself is a good way to recognize success when it presents itself. Therefore, whatever your calling in life may have been, you will recognize that education is the master key.

If remedial action is necessary in terms of education, you have a duty and a responsibility to pursue it. If you happen to be lacking in areas that you believe need upgrading, I strongly suggest remedial actions and assistance.

Principle 2: Don't Run Afoul of the Law.

You probably are aware that young black and Latino men are often the victims or perpetrators of inner-city crime. This plays into the problem of ignorance. In addition, they often make up a disproportional amount of inmates in penal institutions. The reason behind this is clear. This is directly or indirectly linked to poverty and ignorance. Running afoul of the law is a problem. The way to reverse this trend is through education and training.

The first steps in the process begin in the home. Kids who have shown a propensity for violence should receive council very early. They should be taught to talk to authority figures instead of taking matters into their own hands. They should make talk to parents, guardians or teachers. In a school setting, this is even more serious. If your child is hit by another child, your child shouldn't hit back. Instead, the child should complain to the teacher. This dynamic often results in all sorts of problems, including lawsuits. Parenting is serious business, and the task is not for irresponsible people.

I have overheard parents telling their children, especially boys, that they should not be "whoosh." They should not let other kids push them around, and they should learn to defend themselves. I totally disagree with this notion. This is setting the stage for confrontations later in life. You should be aware that the authorities are there to resolve conflicts, dispense justice, and dispensed punishment or rewards. If someone wants to get into a fight with you in the workplace, your duty is to report the matter to your supervisors and not to confront them and take matters into your own hands. This is also true in public and private places. Do not take matters into your own hands.

If you are accosted, you should bring it to the attention of law enforcement. Many confrontations turn deadly. At all costs, try to avoid confrontations with others. Those who run from a fight will live to run from another fight again.

Here are some suggestions for staying out of trouble. It's very easy to get into trouble. You should make sure you are on the right side of the law. You should not steal, and you should not kill, and you should not be involved in any form of contraband. Above all, you should obey the police. Police have authoritative power. They can take you into custody or take your life. As a result, you should not confront the police. That is a big mistake. If the police confront you, you shouldn't resist. Instead, you should fully cooperate. Whatever you do, you shouldn't point a weapon at the police or threaten them.

I often overhear young black men talking to the police. Many people are of the opinion that black men are dumb to confront the police. An honest and upright citizen will do whatever is necessary to stay out of trouble in the first place. One should try to be upright and live an upright life that is behind reproach. I invite my readers and everyone else to be upright. Stay out of trouble, live a peaceful and tranquil life, and avoid the use of opioids and other illegal narcotics.

Principle 3: Stay Away from Mind-Altering Substances

Staying away from all forms of mind-altering substances is the third principle in the series. Everyone will admit that a sober and focused mind is a productive mind as opposed to a mind that is under the influence of narcotics. No one should be altering their minds. If a person cannot confront life without an altered state of mind, there is a problem with that person.

It has been proven many times that addicts often end up in negative situations. As far as children are concerned, this is an unfortunate situation. Young adults have no business experimenting with mind-altering substances. This problem is not limited to the inner cities. It is a gigantic problem across the spectrum. I brought this to your attention earlier.

Many adults are responsible for introducing marijuana and other illegal substances to children, and this is unfortunate. Drugs are paralyzing our people, and this is not acceptable. I believe that people who are responsible for selling illegal narcotics should be put away for life. They aren't friends of the American people in the first place. They are the ones who are helping to dumb down America.

I am concerned about young black men and Latinos with substance abuse problems. Controlled substances of any kind should be avoided. Therefore, my advice is that people should stay away from all forms of mind-altering substances. People who are high on drugs often run afoul of the law, and this is to their disadvantage.

Some people with low morals find it difficult to face the real world without getting high. Drugs are the mask that many are wearing to avoid facing the facts of life. This isn't the appropriate way to go through life. Facing life without the mask is the better way. In that case, they will be able to see things as they are—with a clear and unaltered state of mind. There is no reason to be dependent on external things when one has all the power within. This power is the power that was given to us at birth. This power can solve all our problems. We should be able to get in touch with the power in order to resolve our problems. Remember to do the stillness exercise. This power will guide you to truth and light.

I have witnessed many young adults and older adults who were doing well until they started using illegal substances. Many of these people spiral down to a point of no return. Many lost their jobs, their homes, and their families. Many of them ended up homeless.

Teenage pregnancy is another cause for concern. This is happening across the nation.

Principle 4: Do Not Get Pregnant While in School.

This principle is related to pregnancy of young girls. This affects the parents and the future of those involved. Early childhood pregnancies are problematic at any economic level. This has hit many people in black and Latino communities. Something must be done about this. Education is the answer.

Preventing early childhood pregnancy is the duty and responsibility of parents and guardians. Dropping out of school due to pregnancy is a losing proposition for everyone. As a result, they should discourage early pregnancy and motivate girls and boys to avoid sexual relationships until they are ready to take on the responsibilities of parenthood. This isn't as difficult as it seems. Abstinence will eventually be worth its weight in gold.

Promiscuity should be avoided, especially when it comes to children and young adults who aren't ready to become parents. Sexual activities in young girls and boys is problematic in this country. Poverty begets poverty. We must raise the bar for our children and ourselves.

How can one hope to be respected when one has no self-respect? It's time for young men and women to stop letting their hormones get the better of them. Poverty begets poverty, and this will be a curse on young men and women who must take on responsibilities they aren't ready to handle. The problem of child support is a serious one. The court system is merciless with fathers who refuse to support their children. The question of age will not alter that fact.

The girls are the ones who often suffer the consequences of early pregnancies. Young men aren't exempt. They often suffer the consequences of getting girls pregnant when they aren't ready to take on the responsibility of fatherhood. Due to this problem, poverty and hopelessness are rampant in this nation.

Absent fathers are a contributing factor to poverty, crime, and lawlessness in America. In any event, childhood pregnancy is problematic for young girls and boys—and for their parents and guardians. Due to biological factors, young girls often bear the brunt of this problem. They are the ones who drop out of school. Unfortunately, once they drop out of school, the probability of returning is almost always zero.

There are few exceptions to the rule. All things been equal, this is often the case. If the parent or guardian can step in and provide the necessary financial assistance, this will soften the blow somewhat. In many cases, this isn't the case.

You now understand the consequences of this dilemma. Let's paint the picture more clearly. If a girl gets pregnant at thirteen, fourteen, fifteen, or sixteen, she will probably drop out of school. After the birth, she must stay home for a period of time. The missed time in her education is lost for good. If the girl is lucky to have parents who will see to it that she returns to school, it will be to her advantage. This isn't always the case. In most cases, this young mother will need to fend for herself and her child. You get the picture, don't you?

The girl did not receive a formal education. She has no skills to earn a living. She is at a disadvantage. This is not merely a scenario; these things happen in real life. This is a blemish in many communities across the nation.

Therefore, my advice is that young girls should stay in school and get an education. They should stay away from sexual relationship until they finish school, learn a skill, get married, and are ready to be responsible mothers. This is the message that parents should pass on to their girls. If this was the case, black and Latino communities would be prosperous. There would not be an overwhelming abundance of poverty. We can do much better, and we should start doing better beginning now.

Once again, let me remind you that poverty begets poverty. There are government social programs. Taxpaying Americans are required to shoulder the responsibilities of children who are in poverty. I sincerely hope and pray that our young men and women stop bearing children when they aren't ready and prepared to do so. I know that this is possible. We can do better, and we are going to do better.

This nation is in need of skilled workers. I firmly believe that all people should have at least one marketable skill. We will look into this as we continue.

Principle 5: You Should Acquire Marketable Skills

The final episode in this series is the fact that young adults should acquire at least one marketable skill. The reason behind this fact should be obvious to everyone. This is particularly true in the case of young, urban black and Latino men. I will present the order in which things should be done.

The child should attend school from the elementary level through high school without dropping out. After graduating from high school, the young adult should go to college. This doesn't necessarily mean Harvard, Yale, or Cambridge. If the young adult is able to attend one of these schools, so be it. If this isn't possible, there are other options available. Inexpensive community colleges, technical schools, and vocational schools are all acceptable. The objective is acquiring at least one skill. There are many skills to choose from. This depends on the aptitude of the individual.

After acquiring a marketable skill, the young adult is equipped to enter the job market. The individual can go into business on their own or to seek employment. Either way, a skill of some sort is necessary.

In terms of a relationship, they will probably fall in love. You know the story: "Love and marriage go together like a horse and carriage. You can't have one without the other." This is where the most critical aspects of life come into the equation. Once the young adult ties the knot, children will probably come into the picture.

This is the order that things usually follow in the lives of young adults, but there are exceptions to the rule. There may have been some variation to the process. The important thing is that the individual should get an education, acquire marketable skills, and be gainfully employed before children are brought into the equation. Am I making sense here? The above plan is designed for success.

The point being stressed here is that having a skill will help a person make a decent living and take care of a family. This is not to say that one will not be able to make a living without a profession or skill, but people with skills have an advantage over unskilled laborers.

Other Virtues to Consider

Other virtues and qualities contribute to a successful life. These essential virtues and qualities should be incorporated into a routine for a successful life. Incorporate the following into your daily life: faith, self-control, endurance, love, courage, kindness, patience, and tolerance. If you can't remember all of them, I want you to remember patience. People are inclined to be impatient. They want what they want now. It's as if there will not be a tomorrow. This is certainly not the correct approach to life, and it should be discouraged.

Some people fail to consider the consequences before plunging into things. They fail to look behind the surface and consider the pros and cons before acting. Unfortunately, many of these people end up in the emergency room, the infirmary, the penitentiary, or even the mortuary. There are all sorts of reasons for these dilemmas: bad tempers, mind-altering substances, bad judgment, and disobedience. These are some of the things that can bring regrets for people. If one isn't able to practice the virtues of patience, tolerance, and good judgment, one will achieve nothing—and will likely lose everything.

The next time a thought comes into your mind, please consider it carefully before taking action. Good thoughts and evil thoughts always enter the mind. The mind is always receiving information from the sources of good and evil. It is your duty and responsibility to monitor and act on positive thoughts rather than negative ones.

The Fool Makes Money—Wise People Spend It

They say that the fool makes money, but it is the wise people who spend it. There is profound truth to this proverb. When a person gets in trouble, they might need to see an attorney to regain their freedom. A person who commits a crime will be thrown in jail. To gain his freedom, he will need to see a bondsman. This bondsman will demand payment to secure his release from jail. He will need to solicit the assistance of an attorney to represent him at trial. Now, attorneys aren't inexpensive. Who is the fool, and who are the wise people? Honesty, and uprightness should be embraced. One should be upright in all deportment. When you are honest and upright, you have nothing to fear. That is not to say that trouble will not come. There is trouble on every side in life, but when you are on the right side, you will be victorious every time.

Avoid evil companions and dark passion—and look to Jesus. He will carry you through. Be thoughtful, earnest, kindhearted, and true. Do unto others as you would have them do to you.

The fool makes money, but wise people will spend it. In this case, who is the fool, and who are the wise people?

Before we conclude this chapter, I would like to make it clear that the duty and responsibilities of parents, in terms of a family structure, is more than providing food, clothes, and shelter. They have a duty to bring up their child, or children, in a right and proper manner. If they were not brought up in the proper manner, how will they be able to bring up their children in a proper manner? It may be virtually impossible. This is the type of dilemma facing many people in this county. The time has come to turn things around.

Rich and Famous African Americans

Black people in this country have managed to gain wealth and fame, but they are few and far between. We recognize and salute our brothers and sisters for their contributions to this nation. Unfortunately, there are a few of them who don't invest their money wisely. They often spend the money on unnecessary expensive things. It is as if they are trying to make a statement. This is not the right thing to do. My advice is to assist people at the lower end of the spectrum. There are many ways to help those who are lagging behind: assist them to learning marketable skills, pay their way through college, or assist them in launching businesses in their neighborhoods and communities. Helping people climb the ladder of success would be a win-win situation for everyone. There is a perception that Africans Americans do not help their own people. Is this true? I leave this for you to contemplate and come to your own conclusion. Please help me get this message to the people. The Lord will provide strength for your labor.

This chapter presented information that is of paramount importance to everyone. It will not be necessary to go over it in its entirety, yet some main points should be taken into consideration. Educating oneself is a wise and prudent investment. This should be followed by positive investment in your future. People have approximately forty-five years to work and support themselves and their connections before retirement. This is based on the "three score years and ten" principle. In addition, the ruling class regards the masses as naive. Some of the reasons cited were brought to your attention.

Additionally, five principles for success were presented. I encourage you, if any of the above applies to you, reread this chapter to reacquaint yourself with the information.

This chapter brings motivational assistance to the masses and does not condemn anyone. To cure a dangerous ailment, a dose of strong medicine is needed. I hope you are inspired by this information. Those who are logging behind, you should take advantage of the motivational inspirations.

Remember, the days of our lives are three score years and ten (70 years). Help us, O' Lord, to number our days so that we may apply ourselves to wisdom.

In the next chapter I present to you the Ten Commandments. Ten Commandments are Providential instructions to the human race. In essence, they are boundaries that humans shouldn't cross. Most, if not all of the troubles on this planet, as they relate to humans, are linked to the violation of one or more of the Commandments! If you aren't aware of the Commandments I invite you to study them and govern yourself accordingly!

CHAPTER 9

Providential Command to the Human Race

Humans were given specific instructions by their Creator to keep us on the path to prosperity, success, and happiness. These instructions are nothing more than Providential boundaries that one shouldn't cross. Whenever boundaries are set, we should pay close attention not to violate them. In fact, these Providential Commands are known as "Ten Commandments." From this point on I will refer to them for what they are, the Commandments. They are there to prevent ill will between people. The Creator deemed it necessary to keep the human race in tune with each other. And so He gave us specific instructions.

The Ten Commandments were given to Moses. They were given in order to keep the human race in good standing with our fellow humans and to keep people in good standing with the Almighty Maker. For example, stealing from others is a sure way of bringing vengeance to the offender or offenders. To prevent bringing the wrath of others on us, stealing is forbidden. This is not all. Adultery, among other things, is forbidden. Messing around with another man's wife is a sure way of bringing harm. In order to prevent this breach, the good Lord drew a line forbidding adulterous behavior. I will discuss all of the Commandments in this chapter.

As mentioned, the Commandments were given to us for our own good and to keep us in good standing with others. In terms of worship, the manner in which we should worship the Lord is clearly dictated in the Commandments. The truth is, giving reverence to the Almighty Maker seems to take second place over and above people's duties and responsibilities.

It should be noted that six of the Commandments are dedicated to humans and human affairs. Only four of them are dedicated to the service of the Creator. I will look into other areas as I continue. It should be clear to everyone though, that there are consequences for breaking any of the Commandments. These consequences come in the form of Divine retribution

Let's make a comparison at this point for the purpose of clarification. If a person happened to violate the road traffic regulation — speed limit, stop sign, or whatever it may have been — and this person was not caught and taken before a court of law, this person will go free, from a human prospective.

Assuming that this person ran a stop sign and in the process had taken the life/lives of others, let's assume that the offender went in hiding. The offender is not caught and prosecuted. Whoever this person may be cannot hide from the eyes of Divine Providence. They will pay the consequences for their action.

The point being, there are people who have taken the lives of others, among other crimes. They hide themselves away believing that they will not pay the consequences of their action. They should be aware of the fact that they cannot hide in any place on earth where the all-seeing eyes of Providence will not see. The blood of the departed is on their hands, and sooner or later, misfortune will befall them.

The Commandments are part of an instruction manual or guide that was given to us by the Creator to correct us in our lives.

Please note that manufacturers often provide instruction manuals that show the appropriate way to use and maintain their products. The Ten Commandments are no different. These instructions aren't statics; they are spiritual dynamics. That is why violating any of them will have negative consequences.

The Constitution, for example, is said to be a living, breathing document. The Commandments aren't any different. They are a living, dynamic, spiritual phenomena and should be treated with respect and reverence. They can bring good or evil and punishment or rewards. It's in your best interests to obey them to the best of your abilities. The question of committing adultery is a good example. There are people who have bitterly regretted committing adultery. Many adulterers have lost their homes, families, and even their lives.

And so the Commandments were given as guidelines. They were placed in the Ark of the Covenant, among other things, that Moses brought down from Mount Sinai. They were later stored in King Solomon's Temple in the Holy of Holies, (Sanctum Sanctorum). That's how great a treasure these words of the Creator are. I cannot say enough about the mystery of the Commandments. I want you to understand the dynamics we are dealing with. Please read them and govern yourself accordingly.

If the American people were obedient in keeping Ten Commandments, this nation and its people would not be in this predicament today. We will look at the relevance of the Ten Commandments as they apply to modern ways of life. Most, if not all, problems in this country and across the globe can be traced to disobeying one or more, of the Ten Commandments.

Christians, and others, often question what it was like before the Ten Commandments were given. That is out of the scope of our presentation. One thing is certain and it is that Priovidence has its way in to communicate its message. Instructions probably were delivered through the prophets, kings, and patriots. Providence has ways to communicate its messages and reveal its secrets and mysteries.

All secrets and mysteries that should be known will be made known to the human race. Hidden secrets and mysteries that should be hidden will remain hidden from the human race for eternity. The secrets and mysteries that Providence deems necessary for the benefit of the human race were revealed. Those that should be revealed in the future will be revealed.

Secrets and mysteries relative to the birth of Christ, for example, have been revealed. These secrets and mysteries revealed in this book were given to the human race for the benefit of the human race. And so the secrets and mysteries in connection with the planets in this book should not be questioned in terms of authenticity. They should be accepted for what they are. The Creator of the universe knows his creation far better than we do. Questioning Providence is not in our best interests. Let's continue to dissect the Commandments. I will begin by discussing six of the Commandments that are dedicated to people and their affairs.

Do Not Steal (Exodus 20:15)

As we mentioned previously, taking the possessions of others without consent, forcefully or otherwise, is forbidden. In some cultures, stealing can result in the death penalty. There are many forms in which stealing manifests itself. However, robbery is robbery in whatever form it may take. People who break in and rob often take the lives of their victims. Many people who have broken in to the homes of others have lost their lives in the process. To prevent this, it is forbidden to steal.

There is no need to bring attention to the penalty for taking the life of another person. However, we are currently discussing the problems resulting from stealing. The urge to take others' possessions is strong, and many people have failed miserably in this regard. It should never be forgotten that the urge to steal originates from the nefarious realm. It's wise to monitor our thoughts on a constant basis since the mind is in contact with benevolent and nefarious waves from the universe.

Are planets in the solar system sending harmful waves that are harmful to people? It's not impossible. We are constantly learning about the universe. We will look into this possibility in another chapter.

Stealing often is the result of jealousy and envy, which can be brought about by poverty. However, this is not always the case. There are people who are in poverty, but they will not knowingly steal from others. There are those who are affluent and are guilty of taking things that aren't theirs. Greed is often a factor. Providence, in its wisdom, has given us an instruction manual to keep us in good standing with other people.

Warning, my advice to those who knowingly are involved in stealing is not to continue on this path. I brought to the attention of all my associates, readers, and friends that if anyone has stolen goods in their possession, to return them to their rightful owners. The alternative would be to donate the stolen goods to the Salvation Army. Don't keep cursed goods on your property or on your Person. No one wants misfortune to continue in their homes. He who has ears to hear, let him hear (Matthew 11:15).

Do Not Commit Adultery (Exodus 20:14)

Now, adultery can be painful to the core. Adultery has brought more destruction than anything else: breaking up of homes and families, the division of assets, and the displacing of innocent children. The love triangle syndrome is alive and well in American society, and there is no end in sight. This is another area where nefarious forces are active. Marriage vows often crumble in time. No man wants his wife to have an affair, but he will commit adultery. It is also true the other way around. Women are often guilty of adultery as well.

Now, all is not lost. There are people who are faithful in their marriages. There are people who haven't committed adultery and will never commit an adulterous act. May the Almighty blessing be upon them all the days of their lives.

The rage, bitterness, vengeance, and even bloodshed brought about by adultery is not necessarily all about the sexual activities. It often has to do with the unfaithfulness, betrayal, and insincerity. It results in the loss of two major attributes of a marriage: love and affection.

Adultery contributes to more violence in this country than all the other commandments. People are searching for love and affection regardless of race, religion, or culture. Adultery is like the forbidden fruit. Whoever eats of the forbidden fruit shall surely die. Adultery is destructive to the body, mind, and soul.

Those who are involved in adultery carry scars that produce a sort of halo or dark cloud around them. The scar isn't visible to the naked eye, but it's there. From a biblical point of view, adultery is the only act that allows a man to divorce his wife. If you are involved in the dreadful curse of adultery, please cease and desist immediately. Violating someone's wife or husband is something you don't want to be involved in.

Do Not Murder. (Exodus 20:13)

People were given specific instructions about the things they shouldn't do. Why would Cain take his brother's life? The first known act of murder was the slaying of Abel by Cain. We will look into this story more closely in the next chapter. Unfortunately, nothing has changed since Cain and Abel. In fact, things are getting worse today than never ever!According to Judeo-Christian principles, it's forbidden to take the life of another. However, there are religions that have different points of view on this matter. People who practice religions based on non-Judeo-Christian belief, often take the lives of others as part of their religious belief system. If these people believe that murder is justified, then so be it.

The United States was founded on Judeo-Christian principles. Based on this belief system, we hold the Commandments sacred. If this is the case, then we should not take the life of another human.

Christians and Jews believe that the Ten Commandments are boundaries from a higher power to keep people in harmony with others and to give honor and reverence to the Almighty Maker. "You should not kill" is the instruction that was given to us. Taking anther's life will bring Providential curses in the form of misfortunes to the offender. In fact, breaking any of the Commandment will ensure misfortune in our lives.

Note, the curse that was placed on Cain for killing his brother, Abel, since time memorial is still alive and well. And so, the shedding of blood by one's brother should not come as a surprise to those of us who are grounded in divine truth. Unfortunately, many of those who are murdering cannot help themselves. They are affected by the curse. Since they are at the lower level on the spectrum—morally, educationally, and mentally—we cannot expect better from them. Turning on their brothers probably is an easy option to many of these depraved people.

The fact is, an uneducated mind is a terrible mind. This is not to say that people in the middle class and upper echelons of society don't take the lives of others. Many of them do. Paying attention to the news will verify the authenticity of this statement.

Coveting is another function, like depravity, that should be avoided.

> *Do not covet your neighbor's house. Do not covet your neighbor's wife, his male or female slave, his ox or donkey, or anything that belongs to your neighbor. (Exodus 20:17)*

Coveting means to desire or crave. The desire to take others' possessions, freely or forcefully, has been with people since the Stone Age. This has not changed since then, and that has far-reaching implications. This desire often leads to adultery, robbery, and homicide. Envy and discernment often lead to coveting. "You should not covet your neighbor's possession" is a commandment from the higher power that controls the universe. We are often jealous of people's possessions and successes.

Jealousy and envy are human depravities that often turn into all sorts of nefarious degradation. These problems will always be with people as long as people remain on this planet. There are the haves and the have-nots. There will always be those who are affluent and those who are in poverty. It's not difficult to be jealous of those who have more than us, but we should not be jealous of our neighbors' possessions to such an extent that we want to take it from them by any means necessary. This is easier said than done, I understand, but the penalty will be severe. My advice is to read and govern yourself accordingly.

Greed is a destructive state of mind. The rich are doing all they can to be richer, the middle class is trying to be rich, and those at the bottom are trying to move up to the middle. No one seems to be satisfied with their current standing in life. The more one has, the more one seems to want. This dynamic is playing out across the globe today.

People should try to improve their standing in life, but coveting is not the way to go. One should seek to improve one's standing without stealing, taking the life of another, or committing adultery.

The problem of untruthfulness seems to know no boundaries. Let's discuss this as we continue.

Do Not Give False Testimony against Your Neighbor (Exodus 20:16)

Bearing false witness against your neighbor is forbidden by providential commandments. Bearing false witness is damaging to say the least. In this country, lying is considered perjury. This is a serious offense in eyes of the law and in the judicial system. Lying and bearing false witness often put innocent people behind bars and damage reputations. One should bear in mind that the universe has ears and eyes. We discussed these things earlier. The universe hears every word that anyone speaks. Making false statements and lying will instill misfortune. Lives can, and often are, lost through lying. It isn't uncommon for people to be put to death for things they didn't do due to false witness against them. Because of this depravity, the Divine deemed it necessary to warn against bearing false witness against one's neighbors.

Let's move on to a very interesting subject: father and mother dynamics. In this day and age, children are ruling their parents rather than the other way around. Unfortunately, the government is siding with the children rather than the parents. This is clearly a dilemma facing this nation today.

> *Honor your father and your mother so that you may have a long life in the land that the Lord your God is giving you. (Exodus 20:12)*

Many children are out of control, but their parents do not dare to get mad at them. If you put your hands on a child for disciplinary purpose in this country, you probably will never see the light of day again. Worse, the child will be taken away and placed in the custody of the state, and you will be sent off to the penitentiary for disciplining your own child.

What sort of society is this? We can correct children at home—or they will be corrected in a correctional institution. Which of these options should our society emphasize? As a society, we should determine what course of action we should take. I believe using the rod at home is better than the alternative: a penal institution.

I have presented these six Commandments that are dedicated to people and their affairs. Those of you who are interested in them will find them in Exodus 20. Please remember that we have quoted them from the Holman Christian Standard Bible. Four commandments are dedicated to the honor and glory of the Creator. Please see below.

Do Not Have Other Gods besides Me (Exodus 20:3)

You should worship the Lord, and you should only serve Him. There are people that worship the devil for all sorts of reasons. Whatever the reason, it is clear that people who worship the devil have no lot or part with God. They are known as devil worshipers.

> *Do not misuse the name of the Lord your God, because the Lord will punish anyone who misuses His name. (Exodus 20:7)*

Taking the name of the Lord in vain is something that many people are guilty of. If you didn't know, now that you know, I trust that you will stop this infringement.

> *Remember to dedicate the Sabbath day: you are to labor six days and do all your work, but the seventh day is a Sabbath to the Lord your Good. You must not do any work—you, your son or daughter, your mail or female slave, your livestock, or the foreigner who is within your gate. For the Lord made the heavens and the earth and the sea, and everything in them in six days; then He rested on the seventh day. Therefore the Lord blessed the Sabbath day and declared it holy. (Exodus 20:8)*
>
> *I am the Lord your God, who brought you out of the land of Egypt, out of the place of slavery. (Exodus 20:2)*

These instructions were addressed to the Israelites when they escaped Pharaoh's enslavement in Egypt.

These Commandments are dedicated to the Lord. It's interesting that the Almighty deemed it necessary to provide instructions for people to abide by. As a result, there is no escape from the consequences of violating the Commandments of the Lord.

You will benefit greatly by keeping the Commandments. There are Christians and others who will admit that they don't know or remember the order of the Ten Commandments. As a result, they are presented for your benefit and the benefit of your loved ones.

In essence, the Commandments dictated that you should not do things to others that you wouldn't want others do to you. The wise Creator deemed it necessary to give the human race Ten Commandments as guidelines. You may choose not to revere, worship, or believe in God. Nevertheless, respecting your neighbors and their possessions as presented in six of the Commandments is the right and proper thing to do.

Before we conclude, I would like to remind you that you should be cognizant of the fact that disobeying any of the Ten Commandments has negative consequences. One is sure to pay the consequences in this life—even beyond the grave. No one can hide from the all-seeing eyes of the Lord. Let's endeavor to impress upon the hearts and minds of everyone that—wherever we are and whatever we are doing—the all-seeing eyes of the Lord behold us.

Please note, when the universe is working against people for the wrongs that they have done, under no circumstance should you rejoice over their misfortune! Remember, everyone has to meet their water-loo as they say. If you aren't able to send up a prayer on his/her behalf, you should say nothing. The justice of the Lord is slow but sure.

The presentation of Providential Command, Ten Commandments, is the topic of this chapter. Most of the issues confronting our nation and its people can be traced to people disobeying the Commandments. In addition, overstepping the boundaries designed to keep us in good standing with other people has brought grief on the human race and the American people.

In addition, we highlighted elements from the Commandments that are forbidden—envy, jealousy, greed, adultery, taking the lives of others—which all stem from not adhering to Commandments of the Lord. This nation is supposed to cherish religious and Christian principles, but this is not the case. If this was the case, then why is there so much ungodliness, dispute, strife, and vice? As I mentioned before, the troubles facing this nation are many and varied. Until we get our act together, there is no telling what the future of the next generation of Americans will be.

I sincerely hope that I am helping readers stay on the right path and avoid all forms of conflict, trouble, and danger.

> Please note, the days of our life is three score years and ten,70 years. Help us, O Lord, to number our days so that we may apply our self to wisdom.

Let's take a look at the ring of China to determine what they are doing right. They must be doing great things to be competing with the United States. And so, in the next chapter I will look into the history of the People's Republic of China

CHAPTER 10

The Rising Republic of China

The rising of the People's Republic of China will be the subject in this chapter. Before we continue with China, let's do a brief study of the long history of the People's Republic of China to get a better understanding as to who these people are. Their civilization is far older, and wiser than our civilizations. They have been around for more than 6,000 years, as opposed to ours, under 400 years!

China, "officially the People's Republic of China", is a country in East Asia and is the world's most populated country, with a population of around 1.5 billion people. Approximately 4.6, or almost 5 times the populations of the United States with a population of around 325,000,000. Covering approximately 9,600,000 square kilometers, China is the third-largest country by area. China is located in East Asia, bordering Europe and Africa.

The nation of China emerged as one of the world's first civilizations, in the fertile basin of the Yellow River in the North China Plain. For millennia, China's political system was based on hereditary monarchies, or dynasties, beginning with the semi-mythical Xian dynasty in the 21st century BCE.

One can understand that the Chinese have been around long before the Europeans set foot on the shores of North America. They, the Chines, are awake now, and are rising. Does this mean that their time has come for them to rise in Earnest? Remember, countries rise and countries fall but the earth will abide forever. Whatever the case may have been, Red China is rising and it will soon be on par with the United States before long. Does this mean that the odds are in their favor, and that they will overtake us soon?

China is a one-party socialist republic nation and is one of the few existing socialist states today. Political decisions and human right groups have denounced and criticized the Chinese government saying that humans right abuses, suppression of religious and ethnic minorities, censorship and mass surveillance,and cracking down on protesters such as what happened in 1989, are prevalent.

Since the introduction of economic reforms in 1978, China's economy has been one of the world's fastest-growing with an annual growth rates consistently above 6 percent. In fact, China's GDP grew from $150 to about $12.5 trillion by 2017.

Indeed, the rising China has the highest number of rich people in the world. As a matter of fact, China is on the fast track to becoming the next superpower. This is mainly because of its population of 1.5 billion, its large and rapidly-growing economy, and its very powerful emerging military might.

China's Educational System

Education in China is a state-run system of public education runs by the Ministry of Education. All citizens must attend school for a minimum of nine years. There are more than 100 National Key Universities, including the famous Peking University and Tsinghua University, which are considered to be elite groups of Chinese Universities.

The Ministry of Education reported that a 99 persistent attendance rate for the primary school level, and an 80 percent rate for both primary and middle school. In 1985, the Chinese government abolished tax-funded higher education, requiring university applicants to complete for scholarships based on academic ability and achievement.

In essence, the Chinese people are educated, or are becoming educated. In addition, China has also become a top destination for international studies and ranks third overall among countries where foreigners are going to get an education. This is incredible in my opinion.

I brought these things to light to make a point. The point is that we seem to be lagging behind the Chinese in terms of educating or people. One of my ongoing message is the lifting up of the population, the masses if you will, in terms of education and skill training. Yet, my calling seems to be a lonely voice crying in the wilderness. I will continue to deliver my messages and let the chips fall where they may.

In a capitalistic society such as ours, it's advantageous for the elite the ruling class to keep the masses in darkness and ignorance. By allowing this scourge, they are able to pull the wool over the eyes of the masses. As for those in politics, they are able to take disadvantage by employing all sought of trickery and deception against these masses. Whether or not this nation will be able to change course and return to "the summit" is questionable. In the meantime, Red China is moving to the top while we are engaging in keeping the masses down while preventing this country from remaining at the summit of power and prestige.

The Chinese Economy

China is a global leader in the production of non-metal mineral. The country has an annual production rate of about 97 million tons of phosphate rock. Other valuable minerals produced in China are tungsten, copper, tin and iron. China is also the largest exporter of the world's production. Eighteen percent of its export went to the United States last year. Now, $34 billion dollars' worth of products are subject to a 25 percent of Chinese tariff, forcing some business to expand their manufacture and production outside China. Natural resources of China include but isn't limited to extensive mineral deposit of fossil fuel, water, agricultural products, fisheries, plants and animals. China also has extensive deposits of coal, oil and natural gas.

In fact, that China has lifted more than 800 million of its people out of poverty since the start of its economic reform in 1978 is the greatest story in human history. No other nation has accomplished this feat since the history of man. President Xi Jinping has set specific goals to reach the target: lifting 10 million of its people out of poverty per year between 2016 and 2020,and providing of social safety net for the remaining 20 million poor and infirm who are unable to work. Very, very good for them!

In terms of the workforce, I can understand why many American companies doing business in China find it attractive. The workers are efficient, adaptable, and pay attention to detail. While in this country workers tend to sue for anything and everything. These things are unheard of in China. This is not to say that I am advocating that workers shouldn't stand up for their rights. This trait, however, has turned off many people from doing business in this country and take their businesses overseas: India, Philippines, Mexico, etc.

Religion in China

There are many different religions practiced in China, from Buddhism to ancestor worship,. As a Communist country, China has no official religion. The government does however, officially recognize five religions: Buddhism, Taoism, Islam, Catholicism, and Protestantism.

The government officially espouses state atheism, though the Chinese civilization has historically long been a cradle and host to a variety of the most enduring religion-philosophical traditions of the world.

And so, we see that there aren't much differences between them and us, and other nations in the West in terms of religions persuasion. For example, Catholicism and Protestantism are religions we here in the West can relate to. As for the rest of the religions, I am not educated in their philosophy to comment on them one way or another.

And so, let's find out more about who these Chinese people are.

Who Are the Chinese

The Chinese people are the various individuals or ethnic groups associated with China, usually through ancestry, ethnicity, nationality, citizenship, or other affiliations. The Han Chinese are the largest ethnic group in China, comprising approximately 92% of its mainland population.

Outside of China, the terms "Han Chinese" are also often conflated since those identifying or registered as Han Chinese are the most populous ethnic group in China. In fact, there are about 55 officially-recognized ethnic minorities groups in China who may also identify as Chinese.

Please note, the presentations above may, or may not be accurate. Yet, they don't address the issue in terms of where these people fit from a racial standpoint. Are the Chinese a race of people or are they part of a mixed race? To answer this question, I will turn to biblical history! And so, my intention is to address this issue to clear up any doubt. But first, you should have an understanding of things related to Noah and his wife, their sons, and their wives who survived the deluge when the earth was destroyed by the flood.

Shem Ham and Japhet

Now, people on the earth today are the descendants of Noah's sons. Without presenting the entire story of Noah, I will present excerpts of the story for your information. You may read the entire scriptures for yourself in the book of Genesis.

After the flood Noah and his party were instructed by, the Lord, to go and replenish the earth. Note, Noah's party consisted of: Noah and his wife, their sons, and their sons' wives; Shem, Ham, and Japhet were the names of Noah's sons. To make a long story short, Shem (Semite) is the father of the Persians, (Iranians) the Hebrews (Israelite) and the Syrians, Ham (Amorite) is the father of the Egyptians,and the Ethiopians, and Japhet (Jephite) is the father of the Europeans (Caucasians).

It should be noted that Africa, Asia, and Europe are the continents which were originally occupied and developed by these tribes. And so, people can trace their roots going back to their biblical roots as presented. The Iranians (Persians), Syrians, Hebrews (Israelis) and the Chinese are Asian nations. As such, Shem, Ham, and Japhet are the major racial origins, if you will. However, by reasons of intermingling, and intermarriages, people of many different hues, cultures, and customs came into existence. This has not changed since then. In fact, the mixing of the races across the globe continuing to this day. Because of intermixing, people on the earth have not become extinct since the days of Noah.

In connection with Shem, Ham, and Japhet, there are people who are still question the authenticity of Noah and his wife producing sons with different colors. That is, Ham the dark-skinned, Shem the brown-skinned, and Japhet the white-skinned. My answer to the perplexity is, who can understand the secret and mystery of the Creator and sustainer of the universe? It should be remembered that with the Lord all things are possible!

So the question is, who are the Chinese and where do they fit in the scheme of things in terms of race? Note, the Chinese race weren't mentioned from a biblical standpoint. And so it's reasonable to assume that they are a mixture from the linage of Shem, and Japhet, or Shem and Ham. Remember, the Chinese and the Europeans share a common continent. Europe and Asia are in one land mass. Thanks to the genealogical ancestors of Noah and his sons, and the Divine plan of the wise Creator and sustainer of the universe.

Please note that the story related to Noah can be found in (Genesis Chapter 8:13-17)

Indeed, the Chinese have accomplished a great feat in the Far East. No other nation has built such a massive wall in the history of man. On the other hand, the Egyptians gave the world the Pyramid, the Great Sphinx of Gaza, among other wonders. And so, let's contemplate the Wall of China as we continue.

The Great Wall of China

The Great Wall of China is the collective name of a series of fortification systems generally built across the historical northern borders of China to protect and consolidate territories of Chinese states and empires against various nomadic groups. Several walls were being built from as early as the 7th century B.C.

The Great Wall of China is an ancient series of walls and fortifications, totaling more than 13,000 miles in length, located in northern China. Perhaps the most recognizable symbol of China and its long and vivid history, the Great Wall was originally conceived by Emperor Qin Shi Huang in the third century B.C. as a means of preventing incursions from barbarian nomads. The best-known and best-preserved section of the Great Wall was built in the 14th through 17th centuries A.D., during the Ming dynasty. Though the Great Wall never effectively prevented invaders from entering China, it came to function as a powerful symbol of Chinese civilization's endurance.

Indeed, the Great Wall is one of the wonders of the world and is a great feat for the Chinese. Building the walls probably demanded teamwork, loyalty, and devotion. This sort of cooperation is unheard of elsewhere in the world. And so, we should give the Chinese the credit they deserve.

And so, the Chinese culture are older and wise that ours. They been around for more that 6,000 years, we can learn much from them.

China is rising and is lifting the contentment of Africa in the process. They refer to the Africans as, "our Africans brothers and sisters." Who can have any objection over such good gesture? Europe and the U.K aren't helping Africa notwithstanding the benefits they derive from the continent. In fact, the Europeans and the British has benefited from Africa far more than any other race: they plundered its resources, they gave little, or nothing in return, they shortchanged the people, and failed to invest in the country. These are some of the injustices suffered by Africa and the Africans people by the Europeans and the British people.

JAMES A. HUDSON

China Africa Trade Relationships

Since the founding of the People's Republic of China, China and Africa have developed a long standing friendship. This is advanced by the cooperation in political, economic, and cultural areas. They created a new type of strategic partnership based on political and mutual trust, economic cooperation, and cultural exchanges. In fact, China has demonstrated respect for African countries by actively encouraging cooperation and providing aid between Chinese and African businesses. China is one of Africa's most important trading partners.

When the founding of the People's Republic of China accrued in 1949, it also took the initiative of China-African trade and economic relation. In fact, China seeks resources for its growing consumption, and its 1.5 billion people. African countries, on the other hand, seek funds to develop their infrastructures. As such, large-scale structural projects, often accompanied by a soft loan, were proposed to Africans countries which is rich in natural resources.

I am worried that the Chinese can easily overrun Africa. Although Africa is far larger than China, the population of China are many times the population of Africa. They need each other.

The Chinese seems to be turning to Africa in the hope that they will be benefit from the continent's vast resources. After all, they have so many mouth to feed. And there are lands in Africa lying idle. The coming together would be a win-win for both nations!

On the other side of the spectrum, in the diplomatic and economic rush into Africa, the United States, France and the UK are China's main competitors. In fact, the Chinese surpassed the United States, and all of the above, in 2009 to become the largest trading partner of Africa. In terms of "the rising China," does this sound familiar?

And so, I give you a bird's eye view of some of the things that's taking place in the Eastern (far- east) nation of the People's Republic of China.

We looked into many aspects of the People's Republic of China. We understand that China seems to be on the fast track to becoming the next superpower nation. Remember, countries rise and countries fall, but the earth will abide forever. If it is destiny for China to dominate, people are powerless against this. The rising China is lifting other nations as well. No one can disagree with the Chinese people's willingness to lend a helping hand to their less fortunate brothers and sisters around the globe. This is commendable and they should be credited.

The Mystic East

As the sun rises in the East and sets in the West, so was the gospel promulgated in the East and spread to the West. The Eastern quadrant of the globe seems to sway a mystic spell over the rest of the earth. Whatever Providential afflictions that are intended for the earth probably will come from the Eastern quarter. And so, whatever nation and people Providence chose to propagate a scourge across the globe should not be held accountable. In the case of the Corona Virus that stroked the earth in the year 2020, it is believed to have come out of China. Remember, there must be a source of origination. If China is chosen to be that source, then so be it. The Chinese are doing what they are doing. It's not prudent to cast aspersion on them. Remember, afflictions can originate from any of the four corners around the globe. It should be clear to everyone that the people on the earth are interconnected—we breathe the air that is carried by the East-winds.

The Chinese are interesting people, aren't they? They should be given the credit they deserve. We here in the West may not understand them, yet they are our brothers and sisters. This is based on the fact that we originate from a common biblical parentage as mentioned above. In fact, we aren't even going as far back as Adam & Eve. We fast-forward to the flood in Noah's days. Please note that the deluge of Noah's flood happened sixteen hundred and fifty-eight years of the creation. And two thousand three hundred and forty-eight years before the birth of Christ.

I sincerely hope that you are blessed by the information presented in the chapter.

Before we bring this chapter to its conclusion, I would like to address the issues raised earlier in connection with words of wisdom and inspiration. These words of wisdom and inspiration are presented in the form of poems and chants. Words of inspiration are good for the mind, body, and soul. Many people are writing and sharing poetry for that reason. I hope you will benefit from these words of wisdom as I have benefited from them over the years. As mentioned earlier, these words of wisdom and inspiration are in a novel 5.5x4,38 pages novel that I brought with me from Kingston Jamaica. I received the novel as a gift many years ago. It's the best thing that I ever received. When I am down, I take the novel and recite a few words of wisdom, and the dark shadows/clouds flee. And so I have confidence that you will have a similar experience.

WORDS OF WISDOM AND INSPIRATION

These words of wisdom and inspiration are for you. They will be the best gifts that you could ever receive! Ponder them over and you will feed their deep meanings vibrating deep-within you.

1. Daniel's Band

Standing by a purpose, true and firm, heeding God's command,
honor them the faithful few, all hail to Daniel's Band.
Dear to be a Daniel dear to stand alone dear to have a purpose firm
dear to make it known.
Many mighty men are lost, dreading not to stand, who for God had
 been a host,
by joining Daniel's Band.
Dear to be a Daniel dear to stand alone dear to have a purpose firm
dear to let it known.
Many giants, great and tall, Stalking through the land, headlong to
 the earth would fall
if met by Daniel's Band.
Hold the gospel banner high on to victory grand Satan and his host
 defy,
and shout for Daniel's Band.
Dear to be a Daniel dear to stand alone dear to have a purpose firm
 dear to make it known.

2. Victory over Satan

:Ho, my comrades see the signal waving in the sky reinforcement
 now

appearing, victory is nigh.
See the mighty host advancing, Satan leading on: Mighty men around us are
falling courage almost gone.
Hold the Forth, for I am coming Jesus signals still
wave the answer back to heaven by Thy Grace we will.
See the glorious banner waving hear the trumpet blow in our leader's name
we'll triumph over every foe.
Farce and long the battle rages but our help is near onward comes our Great
Commander, cheer, my comrades cheer.
Hold the Forth for I am coming Jesus signal still wave the answer back to Heaven
by thy grace we will.

3. The Wandering Child

I was a wondering sheep, I did not love the fold: I did not love the
Shepard's voice I would not be control.
I was a wayward child I did not love my home I did not love my father's voice, I love afar to roam.
The Shepherd sought his sheep the Father sought His child they follow me o'er vale
and hill o'er deserts waste and wild:
They found me nigh to death famished and faint and lone, they bound me with the band
of love they saved the wondering one.
Jesus my Shepard is 'twas he that love my soul 'twas he that washed me in his blood
'twas he that made me hole.
I was a wandering sheep I would not be controlled but now I love my Savor's voice
I love I love the fold.
I was a wayward child I once preferred to roam; but now I love my father's voice I love,

I love his home.

3. Yield Not to Temptation

Yield not to temptation, for yielding is sin, each victory will help you
 some other to win fight manfully onward, dark passion subdue
 look
ever to Jesus he will carry you through.
Shunt evil companion bad language disdain God's name hold
 in reverence, nor taken it in vain be thoughtful and earnest,
 kindhearted and true look ever to Jesus he will carry you
through.
To him that Over cometh God giveth a crown through faith we shall
 conquer, though often cast down, but he who is our Savior our
 strength he will renew look ever to Jesus, he'll carry you
through!

4. A Few More Years

A few more years shall roll, a few more season come, and we shall be
 with
those that rest asleep within the tomb:
Then O my Lord, prepare my soul for that great day; Oh wash me in
 thy precious blood,
and take my sins away.
A few more sun shall set o'er these dark hills of time and we shall be
 where suns are not,
a fair serener clime:
Then, O my Lord repair my soul for that blest day; Oh wash me in
 thy precious blood
and take by sins away.
A few more storms shall beat on this wild rocky shore, and we shall
 be where tempest cease,
and surge shall be no more.
A few more struggle here, a few more parting o'er a few more toil, a
 few more tears, and we shall weep no more.

This but a little while, and he shall come again, who died that we might live, who lives that we
with Him might reign; Then, O my Lord prepare my soul for that glad day, oh, wash me in thy precious blood
and take my sins away.

5. Rescue the Perishing

Rescue the perching, care for the dying, snatch them from pity
from sin and the grave; weep o'er the erring one, lift up the falling tell them of Jesus
the mighty to save.
Though they are slighting him still he is waiting waiting the penitent child to receive
plea with them earnestly, plea with them gentle;
he will forgive if they only believe. Down in the human heart, crushed by the temper
feelings lies buried that grace can restore;
if touch by a loving hand awaken by kindness chords that were broken will vibrate once more.
Rescue the perishing duty demand it strength for thy labor
the Lord will provide.
Back to the narrow way patently win them tell the poor wanderer a Savior has died.

6. The Resurrection

On the resurrection morning soul and body meet again no more sorrow,
no more weeping, no more pain.
Here but awhile they must departed, and the flesh its Sabbath keep, waiting in a holy
stillness wrap in seep, eternal sleep.
For a space the tired body lies with feet toward the dawn till there brakes the last and brightest
early on the eternal morn.

But the soul in contemplation utters earnest prayer and song.
Soul and body now reunited henceforth nothing shall divide, waking up in Christ's own
likeness early on that eternal morn.
Oh the beauty, Oh the gladness of the resurrection day which shall not through endless
ages never ever past away.
On that happy Easter morning all the graves their dead restore father, mother,
children brethren meet once more on the eternal shore.
To that brightest of all meetings bring us Jesus Christ at last; to thy cross through
death and judgment, holding fast eternal shore. Amen.

7. Rise Up, Men of God

Rise up, O men of God have done with lesser things: give heart and soul and mind and strength to serve the King of Kings.
Rise up, O men of God his kingdom tarries long; bring in the day of brotherhood and end the night
of wrong.
Rise up, O men of God the church for you doth wait: her strength unequal to her task: rise up
and make her great.
Lift high the cross of Christ tread where His feet have trod, as brothers of the sons of man rise up,
O men of God.

8. Land of Corn and Wine

I've reach the land of corn and wine and all its riches freely mine,
her shines undimmed one blissful day, for all my night has passageway!
O Beula Land sweet Beula Land as on thy highest mount I stand,
I look away across the sea where mansions are prepared for me! And view the shining
glory shore: my heaven, my home my home for evermore.

My Savor comes and walk with me, and sweet communion here have we, He gentle leads me by
his hand for this is heaven's border-land.
A sweet perfume upon the breeze is born from ever-vernal tree, and flowers that, never-fading,
grow where streams of life forever flow.
The zephyrs (east wind) seem to float to me sweet sounds of heaven's melody as Angels with the
white-robe throng join in the sweet redemption song.
O Beulah Land sweet Beulah Land as on Thy highest mount I stand, I look away across the sea Where mansions are prepared for me and view the shining glory shore My heaven, my home for evermore.

9. Time

O God our help in ages past our hope for years to come our shelter from the stormy blast
and out eternal home.
Under the shadow of thy throne thy saints have dwelt secure; sufficient is thine arm alone and our
defense is sure.
Before the hills in order stood, or earth receive her frame from everlasting thou art God to endless
years the same.
A thousand ages in thy sight are like an evening gone short as the watch that ends the night,
before the rising sun.
Time like an ever-rolling stream bears all its sons away; they fly forgotten, as a dream dies at the opening day. O God our Help in ages past our Hope for years to come; be thou our guard
while trouble last and our eternal home.

10. Work while You Can

Work for the night is coming work through the morning hours

work while the dew is sparkling,
work 'mid springing flowers: work when the day grow brighter, work in the glowing sun;
work for the night is coming, when man's work is done.
Work for the night is coming, work through the sunny noon: fill brightest hours with labor,
rest comes sure and soon,
give every flying minute something, something to keep in store: work for the night is coming, when man work
no, more.
Work for the night is coming, under the sunset skies! while their bright tints are glowing work till
the last beam fadeth, faideth to shine no more: work while the night is darkening,
when man's work no more.

11. The Final Journey

When our heads are bowed with who when our bitter tears o' flow
when we mourn the lost, the dearest, gracious Son of May hear.
Thou our throbbing flesh has born, thou our mortal griefs hast borne, thou has shed the human
tear gracious Son of Mary, hear.
When the heart is sad within, with the taught of all its sin; when the spirit shrinks with fear,
gracious Son of Mary, hear.
Thou the shame, the grief has known: thou the sin was not thine own, thou hast deigned their load to
bear; gracious Son of Mary, hear.
When the sullen death-bell tolls for our own departing souls, when the final doom is near,
gracious Son of Mary, hear.
Thou has bowed thy dying head thou the blood of life has shed thou has filled a mortal bier:
gracious Son of Mary, her!

12. If I Have Wounded Any

If I have wounded any souls today, if I have cause one foot to go astray, dear Lord forgive. If I have uttered idle words in vain, lest I myself shall suffer through the stain,if I have walked in my own willful way, dear Lord forgive. Forgive the sins I have confess to thee; Forgive the secret sins I cannot see; O guide me, keep me O dear Lord I pray, dear Lord forgive!

13. Healing Prayer

Angels, or Spirits, of life and health, I ask, renew my body for all it's
    tasks make me strong and full of life,
hear my call and banish strife. Your gift of health I seek to share, hold
    me in your loving care. Nutrients of
the earth will ever be, smoothing protecting surrounding me with
    vital life my body fill, leaving room for no
more Ills, perfect health for all to see, as I will it, so it will be.

    Note, those of you who are sick and are affected and desired to be healed and delivered, pray this prayer reverently with face turn to the East (where the sun rises.) For best results, carried out this prayer until healing take place. And remember, you must believe. Your faith shall made you hold!

A Family Blessing

Lord of all creation, Bless our family. Be they formed by blood or by
    any circumstance,
Make them holy.
May we find you in our relationships. In our marriages, in our
    vocation,
In our households, in our communities, In our global humanity.
May we look across all that divides us, and embrace as a family does.
And love as a family ought to. For where two or three are gather in
    your name, There are you.

CONCLUSION

The United States and the American people are going through troubled times. This is just the tip of the iceberg as they say. As I pointed out, attention should be focused on maintaining our superpower status. For this to be a reality, several conditions must be met. These conditions were brought to your attention. Some of these requirements include educating and training the masses, lifting up the failing, and eliminating the dependencies of Americans on opioids and other mind-altering substances.

Mind-altering substances, among other things, are destroying Americans and America. If these things are allowed to continue, it's only a matter of time before the decline of this nation gains momentum and move into high speed. It will be unstoppable.

I present a mountain of evidence to you. Now, you be the Judge and come to your own conclusion.

The United States seems to have reached its peak. Reaching the peak and remaining at the summit are two different dynamics. Statistics reveal that the United States failed to maintain the latter. That is, failed to remain at the summit of power, wealth, and prestige. And alas, it's descending.

Countries rise, and countries fall, but the earth will abide forever. Indeed, the earth will abide forever but not neatness life on the earth. The conditions for sustaining life on earth must be tolerable. "As long as the earth endures, etc." I brought this to your attention in the chapters of the book!

With all the mess taking place throughout the country, China is rising. Red China will be on par with the United States within decades. Then within a quarter of a century or so, they will surpass us. We the Americans people should take the blame for our failure!

You are already aware of many of the elements contributing to the decline through the chapters of the book. Nevertheless, it is worth mentioning a few before we close. The United States might not be defeated militarily by some external power. The fact is, there are sufficient internal strife, bickering, and unrest to render this nation null and void as a superpower. In fact, this is currently the case! The question of pleasantry between the hierarchy of the two political parties doesn't exist. The same is true with those in the middle, and those at the grassroots level!

There are nations whose people do not like America and Americans very much. They are watching and waiting for this nation to fall into ruins—just as those four fallen ancient empires I brought to your attention did. Certainly, we are playing into the hands of those who don't wish us well.

In terms of poverty, there is unfinished business to be taken care of in this country. The masses are to be educated, marketable skills to be given, and so on and so forth. In addition, impoverished nations could use a helping hand. Instead, we are spending untold amounts of resources preparing for the journey and colonization of distant planets. The fact is, there are Americans who are going without food, clothes, and shelter. This should never be allowed to happen in the United States. How can one explain such breach? What's the reason for all these poverty and homelessness in America?

Many Americans in inner cities and rural areas live in poverty. Poverty and hopelessness are taking their toll, and taxpayers' funds are being investing in voyages to distant planets where people will never be able to live. We are beings of the earth—not of distant planets.

The above are strong indications that decline is taking place. There are lands that can be developed for agriculture purpose. Meanwhile, hunger is common at home and in developing and underdeveloped nations. America has the technology and the resources to make the desert bloom.

People should seek to help other people to eliminate poverty, homelessness, and starvation at home and in impoverished nations that need our help and assistance.

In terms of higher education, not all Americans will be rocket scientists as they say. Nevertheless, those who aren't able to make it to Harvard or other institutions of higher learning should be given marketable skills. This is a shortcoming that should be addressed if America should reverse direction.

To remain on the summit this nation needs scientists, engineers and technicians. The United States should be shipping people in these categories to developing and underdeveloped nations. Instead, the United States is importing people in these categories because many Americans lack these skills.

In the meantime, many wealthy Americans waste their money on politics rather than investing in training the American people for the future. The rich and powerful would rather contribute their fortunes to their favorite political parties than build affordable homes for people of moderate financial means. They could invest in sending deserving people from urban and rural areas to community colleges to learn marketable skills. This would be a win-win situation for this nation and its people.

You are aware of a wealthy New York businessman running for the 2020 presidential election who spent over $357 million of his own money between January and February 16, 2020. Poor inner-city kids could have been helped by this billionaire. He could have assisted the less fortunate kids to go to technical school and learned marketable skills. Yes, he has the right to do whatever he wishes with his money. The question is, should the custodian of material possessions (wealth) not be held accountable for not helping the less fortunate? This businessman is not alone. There are many in this category across the nation!

This nation cannot continue on its current path if it wants to continue to be a first-world nation. The American masses must be lifted up. They must be given first-class education, training, and the ability to invest in the future. The next generation of Americans must be proficient enough to take over and direct the affairs of this nation.

In regard to the universe, you are aware that the universe has a mind of its own. In fact, the universe seems to have ears and eyes. It seems to see us and hear us. Above all, the universe rewards us or punishes us for the things we have done and for the things we fail to do. There seems to be no exceptions. With this in mind, we shouldn't be surprised by the troubles facing this nation and its people.

The fact is, rewards and punishments are constantly in motion. As such, karmic law should not be taken lightly. We will pay conciseness sooner or later for our deeds—be they good or evil. We will reap what we have sown. Many people aren't aware of this karmic law. Ignorance of providential law is no excuse. You must be aware of providential boundaries presented in the Ten Commandments. They are guidelines for keeping people in good standing with other people and the Almighty Maker.

Now, in connection with providential revelations presented in chapter 2, these are cause for concerns. The question of greed and arrogance by humans are well known. Providence proclaimed, these things cannot be allowed to continue, and it will be the elements that will bring about the change, and it will be so.

These revelations go on to mention "overpopulation of the earth, plundering of the seas, pollution of the air", among other things. It's not clear as to what action will be taken to reduce the population of the earth. Could it be by way of plague, famine, incurable disease, or nuclear war propagated by the hands of people? Whichever way, the inhabitants of this planet should take note.

Frankly, there are cases for people on this planet to be concerned with. One thing is certain and it is that when Providence speaks people should listen!

I brought these things to your attention to help you remain true, loyal, and upright. Violating Providential law is one way of bringing divine misfortune. In fact, no one will knowingly bring misfortune on oneself. However, ignorance of the law is no excuse! Pardon me, those of you who are ignorant of the fact, now that you are aware of these things, there is hope for change. In closing, I ask my fellow

Americans to be upright. Be upright in all deportment, knowing that the all-seeing eyes roam through the universe. The all-seeing eyes of Providence behold the good and the evil deeds we have done.

In this life, we will encounter trials that can originate from diverse places. In fact, the long and winding roads of life has brought you to this place. You have won some, you have lose some, but you are here. You have triumphed over every foe! If and when trials and tribulations should reappear, you should remember to bear up nobly under all adversity. Remember, the Lord will provide the strength for your labor if you only believe.

May the Lord bless you and keep you. May the Lord's face shine upon you. May the Lord lift his countenance upon you and give you peace—this day and forever. So be it.

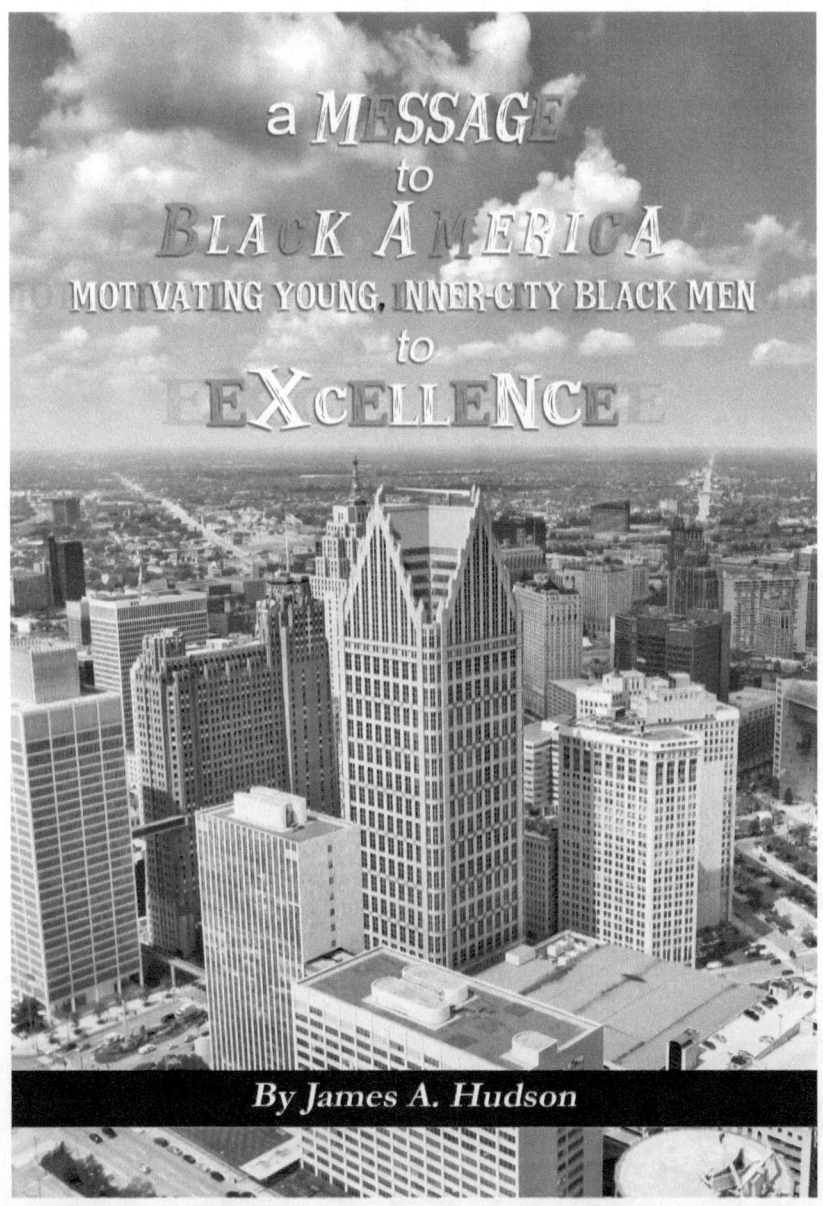

JAMES A. HUDSON

How to Have a Better Relationship with your Mate/Spouse

Better Relationships

James Augustus Hudson

ABOUT THE AUTHOR

James Augustus Hudson was born in Kingston, Jamaica. He came to the United State 1980 and became a naturalized American citizen. His early childhood education was in Jamaica, Roxbury College in Massachusetts, and Cal State Fullerton in California. James is an electronics technician by profession.

He is a gifted visionary who sees and understands things that many others cannot. His vision allows him to solve many problems and offer solutions to problems in the lives of people and things.

This country, the United States, is in trouble. Many of the causes and effects that's contributing to the decline facing this nation and its people are internally generated. Some of them has been brought to your attention in the chapters of the book.

James is the published author of four books: *How to Have a Better Relationship with Your Mate/Spouse*; *Thou Shall Not Kill: What Providence Has in Store for Those Who Do*; *The Rising of Black America with the Assistance of White America*; *A Message to Black America: Motivating Young Inner-City Black Men to Excellence*; and *Dilemmas Facing the Unstated States and Its People: Can We Maintain Our Superpower Status?*

www.ingramcontent.com/pod-product-compliance
Lightning Source LLC
Chambersburg PA
CBHW020530080526
44583CB00013B/809